Cambridge Elements

Elements in Political Psychology
edited by
Elizabeth Suhay
American University, Washington, D.C.

EMPATHY AND POLITICAL REASONING

How Empathy Promotes Reflection and Strengthens Democracy

Lala Muradova
University of Southampton

CAMBRIDGE
UNIVERSITY PRESS

Shaftesbury Road, Cambridge CB2 8EA, United Kingdom

One Liberty Plaza, 20th Floor, New York, NY 10006, USA

477 Williamstown Road, Port Melbourne, VIC 3207, Australia

314–321, 3rd Floor, Plot 3, Splendor Forum, Jasola District Centre,
New Delhi – 110025, India

103 Penang Road, #05–06/07, Visioncrest Commercial, Singapore 238467

Cambridge University Press is part of Cambridge University Press & Assessment,
a department of the University of Cambridge.

We share the University's mission to contribute to society through the pursuit of
education, learning and research at the highest international levels of excellence.

www.cambridge.org
Information on this title: www.cambridge.org/9781009643603

DOI: 10.1017/9781009643573

When citing this work, please include a reference to the DOI 10.1017/9781009643573

First published 2025

A catalogue record for this publication is available from the British Library

ISBN 978-1-009-64360-3 Hardback
ISBN 978-1-009-64361-0 Paperback
ISSN 2633-3554 (online)
ISSN 2633-3546 (print)

Empathy and Political Reasoning

How Empathy Promotes Reflection and Strengthens Democracy

Elements in Political Psychology

DOI: 10.1017/9781009643573
First published online: February 2025

Lala Muradova
University of Southampton

Author for correspondence: Lala Muradova, l.muradova@soton.ac.uk

Abstract: How do individuals make up their mind about politics? This question has sparked a vigorous debate in the study of political behavior for the last few decades. Some scholars contend that citizens can and should engage in political reflection, while others highlight biases in human political reasoning that make reflection impossible. This Element is about the conditions under which citizens can be motivated to transcend their egocentric biases and engage in reflection. Rather than asking whether citizens are capable of reflection, it shifts focus to a more productive question: how to motivate reflection. Firstly, it argues that (situational) empathy for the other side can inspire citizens to think reflectively about politics. Secondly, the Element proposes that deliberative institutions have the potential to evoke empathy for the other side in individuals. Thirdly, it draws on experimental and qualitative data from Belgium, Chile, Ireland, and the UK to test the theoretical expectations.

Keywords: political reasoning, political polarization, empathy, deliberation, citizens' assembly

ISBNs: 9781009643603 (HB), 9781009643610 (PB), 9781009643573 (OC)
ISSNs: 2633-3554 (online), 2633-3546 (print)

Contents

1 Introduction

How do individuals make up their minds about politics? This question has sparked a vigorous debate in the study of mass political behavior for the last few decades. Some scholars contend that citizens can and should engage in political reflection, while others highlight the biases in human political reasoning that make reflection impossible. This Element is about the conditions under which citizens can be motivated to transcend their egocentric biases and engage in reflection.

Normative democratic theorists expect citizens to engage in *reflective political thinking*, whereby they consider and assimilate diverse and opposing viewpoints into their thinking, weigh up the pros and cons of an issue or a candidate, and reexamine their prior beliefs when forming their political beliefs and attitudes. Aristotle posited that individuals' political judgments should be the product of "determined effort, a pausing-and-reflecting, and a self-distance," as opposed to "spontaneous, immediate intuition" (Beiner 1983, 105). In Reflective Democracy, Robert Goodin argues that people should think "long and hard what they want and why [. . .], what others want and why, and how those others' goals might articulate with their own" (2003, 1). For Arendt, critical political thinking "is possible only where the standpoints of all others are open to inspection" (Arendt 1989, 43). Reflection, according to John Dewey, is the hallmark of democratic citizenship (Dewey 1933).

However, there is a widespread pessimism about the capability and willingness of voters to reflect. This skepticism stems from empirical evidence in political science and psychology. Research finds that most people rarely think about opposing perspectives, and when faced with opposing information, they react defensively by clinging to their existing attitudes and beliefs (Taber and Lodge 2006). People's emotional attachment to their favored political party makes them support their party and endorse party positions, irrespective of whether these positions reflect citizens' policy preferences or not (Bartels 2002). This strand of literature concludes that prior political beliefs and social identities predetermine and shape people's political beliefs and policy choices.

Those findings prompted some critics to argue that there is a disjuncture between the normative conceptions about how citizens *should* reason, and empirical research on how citizens *do* think (Achen and Bartels 2016; Campbell et al. 1960; Converse 1964). Pointing to empirical findings that citizens have biased, "thin, disorganized and ideologically incoherent" belief systems (12), Achen and Bartels (2016) argue that the normative democratic theory, in particular, its deliberative conception, is "unrealistic," "populist," "romanticized," and "folk"; and "amount[s] to fairy tales" (7). But such an argument about the "insurmountable" divide may be overly simplistic, as suggested by a growing body of recent work on the psychology of political opinion formation (e.g., Groenendyk and Krupnikov 2021).

In this Element, I take a different approach to political reasoning. Rather than asking whether citizens are capable of reflection or not, I focus on a more productive question of *how to motivate citizens to engage in reflective political thinking*. I draw on insights from contemporary political psychology to start with an argument that human political reasoning is dynamic, rather than static (see also Esterling et al. 2011). Different situational factors can either enhance or depress people's motivation to engage in reflective political thinking. People should be "sufficiently motivated" to engage in even-handed political thinking (Druckman 2012, 199). The tendency to engage in reflection "depends on the goals made salient by the context of politics" (Connors, Pietryka, and Ryan 2022; Groenendyk and Krupnikov 2021, 181).[1] Altering people's motivations, by holding them accountable (Colombo 2018), making the value of open-mindedness salient (Groenendyk and Krupnikov 2021), paying them to be accurate in their judgments (Bullock et al. 2015), or reminding them about their civic duty (Mullinix 2018) have shown to engender better, and normatively more desirable political thinking. Intense political campaigns (Kam 2006) and televised election debates (Turkenburg and Goovaerts 2024) have the potential to start similar reflective thinking processes in citizens. I build on this literature and expand it with novel theoretical arguments and new empirical evidence.

First, I theorize about the motivating force of *empathy for the other side* for *reflectiveness of people's political reasoning*. In a nutshell, I argue that empathy can promote political reflection. In building my argument, I focus on *situational* empathy (empathic reactions and states in response to a specific situation and/or to a person), rather than *dispositional* empathy (a character trait). Given that individuals often lack self-awareness about their empathic abilities (Ickes 1993, 2003) and that empathy is a motivated response (Zaki 2018), I argue that situational empathy is more suitable for studying its democratic effects. In short, I contend that *when individuals are encouraged to imagine the world from different others' vantage point and feel empathy for the other side, they are motivated to move beyond their egocentric political thinking and engage in more reflective political reasoning.*

Second, I offer theoretical insights into the kind of *political institutions* that are capable of evoking empathy for the other side in citizenry. I develop an

---

[1] Research shows there are also individual-level characteristics that make people either more or less willing to process political information in a reflective manner (e.g., Arceneaux and Vander Wielen 2017; Bakker et al. 2020; Valli and Nai 2023; see Muradova and Arceneaux 2022a for a review of the literature). Engaging with this literature, however, falls outside of the scope of this Element.

account of how and under what conditions *deliberative institutions* have the potential of providing a fertile environment that facilitates the kind of affective engagement that enables citizens to connect with each other and experience empathy for the other side. This elicited empathy motivates individuals to reflect about their political judgments. In developing my argument, I focus on structured deliberative forums, because these approximate the ideals of democratic theorists through their design. Lastly, I explore the upscaling potential of interpersonal deliberation.

I test my theoretical expectations through the examination of diverse policy issues, such as abortion, assisting aging populations, climate change, legalizing assisted dying, and universal basic income, using a mix of experimental, quasi-experimental, and qualitative data collected from Belgium, Chile, Ireland, and the UK.

This Element speaks to different strands of literature within political psychology and deliberative democracy. First, the findings have implications for the contemporary political psychology and communication literatures on political reasoning, emotions, and attitude formation. It adds to the motivational theories of political reasoning by showing that empathy for the other side can create a motivation for individuals to engage in more reflective political reasoning. The findings are consistent with the argument advanced by George Marcus and others about the motivating role of some emotions for the deliberativeness of political reasoning (Marcus et al. 2000; Webster and Albertson 2022). Prior literature examined the role of different discrete emotions, such as anxiety, anger, and enthusiasm in individuals' political reasoning, showing the ways via which anxiety can lead to more enlightened political judgments. For the first time in the literature, I argue about and study the motivational effect of another emotion, *empathy*, for reflectiveness of people's political reasoning. I show that when a political environment triggers empathy for the other side in individuals, this elicited empathy engenders more reflective political reasoning in individuals.

The findings of this project also hold important implications for the recent political science literature investigating the role of empathy in politics (Clifford et al. 2019; McDonald 2023; Simas et al. 2020; Sirin et al. 2016, 2021). This work has broadly fallen into two distinct camps: (a) the studies that investigate empathy as a disposition (a stable, trait-level characteristic), and (b) the studies that examine the effect of perspective-taking interventions, that is, those that focus on cognitive dimension of empathy. My contribution to this field is (at least) two-fold. First, contrary to studies suggesting that individual-level *dispositional* empathy is biased against outgroups (Brophy and Mullinix 2024; Simas et al. 2020), I demonstrate that *situational empathy* toward the opposing side enhances the reflectiveness of political judgments by motivating individuals to actively entertain counter-attitudinal arguments and perspectives. Similarly, in contrast to Paul Bloom's (2017) argument that (affective) empathy leads to irrationality, this Element suggests that situational empathy can prompt individuals to engage in more (not less) thoughtful reasoning. This finding challenges the notion that empathy inherently distorts judgment. While dispositional empathy may have detrimental consequences for the quality of democracy, motivating individuals to be empathetic – regardless of their personal traits – holds normatively optimistic potential for fostering reflective democratic citizenship.

The findings of this Element align with research showing that perspective-taking interventions can help reduce outgroup biases (Broockman and Kalla 2016; Kalla and Broockman 2023) and diminish attitude entrenchment (Tuller et al. 2015). I demonstrate that empathy promotes greater reflection, even if it doesn't always result in persuasion.

Second, the results have implications for the field of deliberative democracy. I propose a theory of deliberation that links affective engagement and the resulting empathy for the other side in interpersonal deliberative settings to normatively desirable political judgments. In doing so, I attend to the affective dimension of interpersonal deliberation (Krause 2008; Morrell 2010; Rosenberg 2007), and I contribute to filling in the gap identified by Michael Neblo (2020, 926) that "the theories of what roles emotion can and should play [in interpersonal deliberation] have been underdeveloped" within deliberative democratic literature. This focus also speaks to an incipient body of theoretical and empirical work on the role of emotions in deliberation (Curato 2019; Lacelle-Webster 2024; Landemore 2024; Muradova 2020; Penigaud 2024; Saam 2018).

The Element has seven sections and proceeds as follows. The subsequent section (Section 2) articulates the theoretical framework that informs this Element. I start by conceptualizing reflective political thinking and differentiating it from other similar concepts. Next, I position my model of political reasoning within the latest research that places emotions at the heart of political information processing and belief formation. In Section 3, I discuss the operationalization and measurement of two concepts central to this Element: reflective political reasoning and empathy. I further elaborate on the analytical strategy adopted in this Element. I briefly describe all five empirical studies testing different parts of the theory. Section 4 presents the findings of a large and nationally representative survey experiment in the UK (Study 1, UK), which tests my first theoretical argument (i.e., "empathy motivates more reflection," H1). This study manipulates empathy for the other side in the context of a political disagreement on the issue of introducing universal basic income and studies its effect on the reflectiveness of individuals' political reasoning. In Section 5, I undertake an empirical inquiry to test the theoretical expectation about the potential of deliberative institutions to elicit empathy for the other side in individuals (H2), focusing on a real-world structured deliberative institution, the Irish Citizens' Assembly (Study 2) and relying on qualitative in-depth interview data, and participant observations. In Section 6, I substantiate my findings from the Irish Citizens' Assembly with a quasi-experiment (Study 3, Belgium) and a laboratory experiment (Study 4, UK) on small-group deliberation about the issue of legalizing assisted dying (H3). I further investigate the upscaling effect of interpersonal deliberation on reflection through a survey experiment focused on the issue of universal basic income (Study 5, Chile, and the UK). Section 7 summarizes the Element's main contributions and discusses the ways via which reflective political reasoning can strengthen democracy. I then devote the remainder of the section to discussing the limitations of my empirical studies and pondering over the future avenues for research.

2 Theory: Empathy, Deliberative Institutions, and Reflection

2.1 Conceptualizing Reflective Thinking

Reflective political thinking happens when one uses their thinking processes to consider and integrate diverse and counter-attitudinal information and perspectives about an issue or a political candidate, before forming their political attitudes. Reflection involves the willingness to go beyond one's existing beliefs and group identities and evaluate political information in an even-handed and deliberative manner. To conceptualize "reflection," I build on normative democratic theories about the ideal citizenry (Arendt 1989; Dahl 1971; Dewey 1933; Goodin 2003; Habermas 1996) and the definition of reflection adopted by Arceneaux and Vander Wielen (2017). A crucial defining aspect that characterizes "reflection" in my project is its "other-regardingness": at its center is the willingness to contemplate the perspectives contrary to one's own (Muradova 2020).

What distinguishes "reflection" from other similar concepts in the field? Reflection involves more than just thinking hard. Thinking hard about political information and perspectives could be done in service to one's prior preferences. Individuals can think hard to produce post hoc rationalization for their unreflective and intuitive judgments (Arceneux and Vander Wielen 2017). Reflection is the act of actively entertaining not only the perspectives and arguments that support one's stance, but especially those that oppose it. Quoting philosopher Robert Goodin, reflection involves "taking due account of the evidence and experience embodied in the beliefs of others" (2003, 1).

Reflection is also distinct from critical reasoning. Both reflection and critical reasoning require a skeptical mindset when evaluating political information at hand. Yet reflective reasoning extends past mere skepticism, involving an active consideration and incorporation of different and opposing perspectives on the issue or the candidate.

The concept of reflective thinking shares similarities with the concept of accuracy-motivated reasoning. According to the influential *motivated reasoning* framework, individuals are driven by different goals when processing political information. Two main motivations guide people's political reasoning. The default goal is directional. Political reasoning is directional when individuals are motivated by a goal of protecting their prior beliefs and partisan identities. When motivated directionally, people process and evaluate new information through the lens of their existing beliefs and/or partisan attachments. This motivation leads individuals to seek out arguments that align with their existing beliefs, while deliberately ignoring those that challenge them (Taber and Lodge 2006). In my conceptualization, directionally motivated reasoning stands in opposition to what constitutes "reflective reasoning." When engaging in directionally motivated thinking, individuals do not consider or integrate the perspectives of those they disagree with. Neither are they willing to reconsider their previously held views on a political issue. Their affective attachments to their prior beliefs and political partisanship drive their political attitude formation. Conversely, when individuals are motivated by accuracy goals, they strive to develop a belief or attitude that can be considered the most correct or optimal (Kunda 1990; Taber and Lodge 2006, 756). Accuracy-motivated political reasoning, thus, is similar to reflective thinking. Yet the former fails to fully encapsulate the essence of the latter. Reflection goes beyond achieving accuracy in political judgments. Reaching accurate judgments may not always be attainable or relevant. It could be conceptually and empirically much easier to apply "accuracy" to the matters of fact, but less so to the matters of morality, where different, more other-regarding considerations should come into play. Moral issues involve complex and nuanced considerations of values, norms and ethics, and the goal of attaining accurate judgments on such issues may be elusive (if possible, at all). To illustrate this, consider this (simplified) example about attitude formation on legalizing assisted dying. Person A holds a belief that it is individuals' right to decide to die on their own terms, particularly if they suffer from a terminal illness and, therefore, supports the legalization of assisted dying. Person B is against legalizing assisted dying and is convinced that its legalization would put vulnerable parts of the population, such as the elderly and those with physical and mental needs, at risk of coercion and pressure. When motivated to think reflectively about legalizing assisted dying, Person A should actively consider and integrate Person B's opposing perspective. The goal here, however, is not accuracy, which is impossible, but more reflective judgments.

Another distinct feature of reflection is its nonlinear relationship with attitude change. I believe this is what makes reflection normatively more desirable than mere persuasion. Reflective political reasoning offers an opportunity for a shift in beliefs and/or attitudes, though the change is not always the ultimate outcome of reflection (Muradova and Arceneaux 2022b, 741). At times, upon hearing the opposing argument/viewpoint and reflecting upon it, an individual may decide to update their prior beliefs in the direction of a new piece of information. In other instances, reflection may ultimately reaffirm one's initial beliefs or even strengthen them. Reflection may also encourage behavioral change without transforming people's beliefs.[2] Furthermore, while observable transformation of attitudes may capture attitude change post-exposure to an intervention, reflection may yield changes in beliefs and attitudes in the longer run. Reflection can also increase future openness and tolerance to opposing views without immediately altering one's existing beliefs. Finally, the outcome of reflection may not warrant any change in people's political attitudes, either short- or long-term. I believe all these outcomes are democratically valid, as far as they are the result of reflective political reasoning.

2.2 Empathy for the Other Side Engenders More Reflective Political Thinking

The main argument guiding this Element is that empathy for the other side has the potential to enhance the reflectiveness of people's political judgments. Before laying out my argument, however, it is important to elaborate on the definition of "empathy" adopted in this Element. The term "empathy" is a definitional morass.[3] Empathy means different things to different people in different disciplines, leading some scholars to argue that empathy is a layered, umbrella concept (de Waal 2012), encompassing a range of interconnected emotions, such as sympathy, empathy, compassion, and emotional contagion, among others.[4]

In this Element, consistent with the most recent literature, I define empathy as a multidimensional concept, having both affective (feeling) and cognitive (imagining and understanding) components that occur together, interact with

---

[2] I illustrate this point empirically with an example in Study 2.

[3] The expression of "definitional morass" comes from Gerring (2004).

[4] Due to space restrictions, I'm unable to discuss the vibrant contemporary debate about the definition of empathy. For comprehensive and interdisciplinary reviews on empathy, see Decety (2012) and Stüber (2019).

each other, and work in synch (Cikara et al. 2011). Empathy is thus defined as "actively imagining, feeling and understanding the world from the other person's vantage point" (Muradova and Arceneaux 2022b, 743). Even though empathy has a motivational cognitive component ("actively putting yourself into someone else's shoes"), it also includes affective reactions of sympathy and compassion to the target (whose perspective one is taking) and to their emotional experiences (Sirin et al. 2016). I argue that these affective reactions, together with the parallel processes of understanding where the target is coming from, influence and motivate our reasoning.

In building my argument, I depart from previous research and focus on *situational empathy*, defined as a "situational [empathic] response in specific situations" (Stüber 2019), rather than a dispositional one. I build on the premise that social contexts can either activate or depress people's empathic reactions, with some contexts exerting a strong influence on individuals' inclination to empathize with others (Cheng et al. 2017). Lastly, my focus here is on empathy targeted toward political opponents, people whom one disagrees with on political matters, which I call *empathy for the other side*. Empathy for the other side thus entails imagining the feelings and perspectives of someone who does not share one's political views on a given issue.

However, actively imagining the world from the vantage point of someone who doesn't share our political views may be challenging and come with inherent biases and barriers. For instance, we may be more predisposed to be empathetic toward people who share common characteristics or backgrounds with us. I argue that, for empathy for the other side to happen, at least three conditions need to be met.

The first necessary condition is for the *individual to be actively willing to engage in empathy* – "to put themselves in the shoes of the other," figuratively speaking. Empathy is not automatic. It requires a personal commitment to engage in such a process. Different situational and institutional factors can create a motivation in individuals to engage in empathy for the other side. In experimental settings, specific empathy instructions could play this motivational role.

Second, for an individual to imagine the world of the other, *they need to have enough and accurate information about that world* (Muradova 2020). The lack of information may lead the individual to make erroneous inferences about the lives and experiences of the target of their empathy, reinforcing their biases. In the absence of information about the other side, an individual may automatically rely on their stored knowledge, which may consist of "stereotypes or other idiosyncratic information known about the target" (Epley and Caruso 2009, 300–305; Muradova 2020).

Third, empathy requires an *activation of people's affective empathic reactions,* not only their active willingness to take a perspective. Empathy as a multidimensional emotion incorporates both cognitive (actively putting oneself into someone else's shoes) and affective (the feelings of warmth and concern felt toward the other) dimensions and the two are intertwined and work in tandem. Communicating the other's world (including perspectives, arguments, and feelings) in a way that facilitates the process of affective empathy for the other side is crucial. Personal stories and narratives are strong discursive tools for encouraging affective empathy and imagination in individuals (Black 2008; Muradova et al. 2020). They bring in an affective piece of information which is helpful in the processes of imagining the other's world (Black 2008).

In sum, actively imagining the world from the perspective of a political opponent, after having read/seen/heard about their perspectives and feelings, in a narrative format, facilitates the processes of empathy for the other side.[5]

This argument about the power of empathy to promote reflection builds on the prior literature that posits that emotions are consequential for humans' willingness and tendency to process political information and reason about politics in a more deliberative way (Brader and Marcus 2013; Marcus 2010). Much of this research has confirmed the existence of the dual-process models of reasoning. In these accounts, political reasoning is the outcome of two interlinked processes, the intuitive (automatic or system 1) and the deliberative (rational or system 2), and emotions are involved in both processes (Arceneaux and Vander Wielen 2017). The default mode of reasoning for individuals is to rely on their habits when making political decisions unless something novel shakes their default system. George Marcus, in developing his Affective Intelligence Theory (AIT) argues that one discrete emotion, anxiety, can act as a motivator for more deliberative political reasoning, by prompting individuals to stop relying on their habitual thinking and search for more diverse information. Enthusiasm

---

[5] My conceptualization of *empathy for the other side* has some similarities with the concept of *perspective-getting*, proposed by Kalla and Broockman (2023). The authors make a distinction between perspective-taking (where one self-generates a narrative about the life of an outgroup member) and perspective-getting (when an individual hears a narrative about a life of an outgroup member either from them directly or from a third party). Both concepts (empathy for the other side and perspective-getting) incorporate the narrative format and information about the experiences of the different other. Perspective-getting is only one aspect of empathy, with other dimensions involving affective engagement with the feelings, perspectives, and life experiences of others, which are important for its reflection-inducing motivation. Hence, while Kalla and Broockman (2023) focus on perspective-getting, my argument includes both the cognitive and affective dimensions of empathy, examining it in its entirety. Moreover, according to my conceptualization, all forms of empathy require information about the other side; without it, our potentially flawed perceptions can impede our ability to empathize effectively.

and anger, on the other hand, are argued to prompt more intuitive and biased political reasoning. There is an increasing body of work that shows that anxiety is linked to people's tendency to seek more information, rely less on party identification or ideology as a heuristic and consider the characteristics of policy proposals and candidates when making political decisions (Brader et al. 2008; Gadarian and Albertson 2014; Huddy et al. 2015; Marcus et al. 2000). I argue that empathy, more specifically *empathy for the other side*, can start similar reflective processes in individuals. When the cues in the environment elicit empathy in individuals toward people with opposing views, the resulting empathy signals them to stop relying exclusively on their default system of reasoning and engage in more even-handed thinking. In the language of AIT, empathy acts as a trigger for individuals' surveillance systems, prompting them to go beyond their egocentric reasoning. Empathy, therefore, disrupts our habitual patterns of political thinking and encourages us to consider opposing perspectives and arguments. I argue that the arousal of empathy for the other side can activate and engender more reflective political thinking.

This argument is in line with the findings of social and political psychological research that shows empathy has the potential to reduce explicit and implicit intergroup biases at the individual and group level (Simonovits et al. 2018; Sirin et al. 2021), foster more inclusive and altruistic behavior (Batson 2010; Todd and Galinsky 2014), lead to transformation of political views (Tuller et al. 2015) and influence political ambition (Clifford et al. 2019).[6] I extend this body of work by studying how situational empathy is related to people's tendency to engage in a more demanding and normatively desirable kind of political reasoning, *reflection*.

Several causal mechanisms could be responsible for the relationship between empathy for the other side and reflection. First, the argument on *self-other merging* in empathetic imaginings suggests that empathy can create a sense of psychological connectedness between individuals (Todd et al. 2012, 739) and help them recognize shared similarities and fates with the person whose perspective they are adopting (Erle and Topolinski 2017). Consequently, one may perceive oneself as being more like the other and/or vice versa. Second, empathic imaginings could activate more positive evaluations of others, and more liking (Galinsky and Moskowitz 2000). This may lead to openness about the arguments and perspectives of different others. Therefore, when political environments are fertile for eliciting empathy in individuals toward those with divergent political views, people would be more likely to engage in reflective reasoning.

---

[6] The source of empathy-related interest in psychology dates to the moral philosophy of the eighteenth century and is inspired by the works of David Hume and Adam Smith. For a discussion of the history of scholarly interest in empathy, see Stüber (2019).

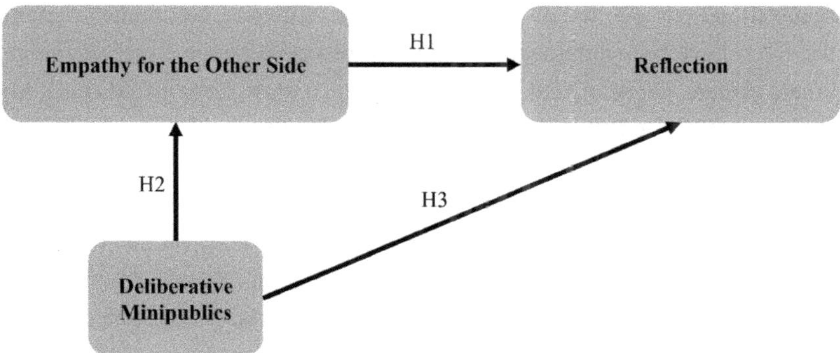

Figure 1 Schematic representation of the hypotheses

This argument leads us to expect that **empathy for the other side would motivate more reflective political reasoning in individuals (H1)**. Figure 1 lays out this and other proposed relationships.

2.3 Political Institutions that Induce Empathy for the Other Side

How to make people more empathetic toward different others, outside the controlled experimental settings? How can political institutions help individuals to feel empathetic toward their policy opponents and consequently, engage in more reflective political reasoning?

The second main argument of this Element is that one type of institutions – deliberative minipublics – have the potential to elicit empathy for the other in individuals. Minipublics are nonconventional, non-electoral and participatory institutions that approximate the ideals of deliberative democracy through their design (Fung 2003). They are considered to be the microcosm of the larger population that they represent. Minipublics bring together randomly chosen citizens with diverse views to hear from the experts and witnesses, engage in consideration, discussion, and deliberation about the chosen issue, and arrive at a set of recommendations under the conditions of respect and equality (Curato and Farrell 2021). The assumption underlying these institutions is that a minipublic models "what the electorate would think if, hypothetically, it could be immersed in intensive deliberative processes" (Fishkin 1991, 81).

There are different types of minipublics (e.g., citizens' juries, consensus conferences, citizens' assemblies, and deliberative polling) and their political influence differ from case to case.[7] The organization and use of a specific type of minipublic – citizens' assemblies – by governments and nongovernmental

---

[7] See Ryan (2021) for the discussion and policy impact of another type of democratic innovations, participatory budgeting.

organizations worldwide have been on the rise. Citizens' assemblies (herein-after CAs) have been employed to tackle various contentious issues, including climate change, abortion, and same-sex marriage (www.participedia.com). My argument in this section refers to citizens' assemblies, considered to be "demo-cratically superior" to other deliberative institutions (Elstub 2014, 172), with larger number of participants (usually around 100), longer period of deliber-ations, and a more established link to the conventional political institutions.

I argue that participation in a deliberative institution can make people more empathetic toward the other side, which is consequential for the reflectiveness of their political judgments. One explanation of this relationship could be found in intergroup contact theory. Originating in social psychology, the contact theory contends that intergroup interaction has the potential to promote positive intergroup outcomes, such as reduced anxiety, lower levels of physiological stress, and enhanced empathy in addition to its more widely known outcomes, such as reduction in prejudice and conflict between groups (Allport 1954; Pettigrew and Tropp 2006; Pettigrew et al. 2011). In *The Nature of Prejudice*, Allport (1954) posits that for intergroup contact to have positive effects it should meet four important conditions: (a) equal status of interacting groups in the situation, (b) common goals, (c) intergroup cooperation, and (d) the support from the authorities, law or custom. Even though these conditions are not always necessary (Pettigrew et al. 2011), their presence facilitates and increases the beneficial effects of contact with different others. A minipublic looks like mediated intergroup contact. Instructions given by the organizers to the members of the minipublic are intended to encourage cooperation between people holding opposing perspectives, foster equal status, and motivate them to work toward the common goal. Minipublics also offer institutional support to deliberating individuals (Fishkin et al. 2021).[8] Thus, minipublics are institu-tions that create necessary institutional conditions for individuals to engage in positive intergroup contact.

However, in building my theoretical expectations about the relationship between interpersonal deliberation in minipublics and empathy for the other side, I go beyond intergroup contact theory and theoretically unpack affective processes that encourage and facilitate empathy for the other side in deliberating individuals.

When designed well, minipublics create a positive and safe space for individuals of different background and perspectives to engage *affectively* with each other and with each other's lives and perspectives. In Jane Mansbridge's words (1983, 5),

---

[8] The argument and the empirical studies in this Element study contact with different others; but the difference here is defined across political beliefs and attitudes, rather than social group memberships.

face-to-face discussions in such settings inspire individuals to "identify with one another and with the group as a whole" (Mansbridge 1983, 5), leading to co-creation of shared goals and aspirations. This co-creation of common goals happens in a social context, where human emotions take a central stage. Spending time together within deliberative groups and beyond, for extended periods of time, encourages individuals to form more intimacy with different others and fosters overall trust and social bonding (Rosenberg 2007). On one hand, this affective engagement would encourage people to share their lives and experiences more openly. These exchanges of personal stories and perspectives would provide the individuals with the necessary information to empathize with the lives of others who were previously distant. On the other hand, affective engagement can foster a positive affinity for political opponents – those with differing political perspectives – and encourage openness to learning about their lives. As Diana Mutz (2002, 112) contends, "one could learn from personal experience that those different from one's self are not necessarily bad people." Through affective engagement and social bonding, minipublics create favorable physical and discursive spaces for two necessary conditions for practicing empathy for the other side: (a) sufficient and accurate information about the other, and (b) affective empathic elicitation via narratives and personal stories. Emotional proximity and interpersonal linkages facilitate the expression of such information by different others and enhance participants' receptivity to it. Social bonding also leads people to be open to telling personal stories from their lives. Moreover, the institutional design of deliberative minipublics encourages individuals to engage in empathic imagination. From the outset, organizers urge citizen deliberators to remain open to the lives of others, inspiring them to actively empathize with opposing perspectives. In sum, *deliberative minipublics are institutions that through their design create an environment that facilitates and harnesses the feelings of empathy for the other side.*

This argument contributes to the previous work within deliberative democracy that emphasizes the role of empathy for deliberation. Michael Morrell's (2010) influential book *Empathy and Democracy* calls for reimagining and reshaping deliberative democracy by placing empathy at its heart. For many deliberative democrats, empathy is a deliberative virtue with the potential to promote inclusiveness (Krause 2008) and strengthen mutual respect and reciprocity (Morrell 2010; see also Richards et al. 2022). While deliberation literature has either implicitly or explicitly referred to empathy in talking about interpersonal discussion, there is a dearth of research that links deliberation to empathy both theoretically and empirically. There are, however, some notable exceptions. Grönlund and colleagues (2017) study the extent to which deliberation in small groups improves people's capacity to empathize with others on the issue of immigration. In their experimental study design, they manipulate whether deliberation is "enclave" (deliberation with like-minded people) or "cross-cutting" (deliberation with different others). The findings show that deliberation increases outgroup empathy among individuals with restrictive attitudes toward immigration. In a highly divided political context, relying on an experiment in Colombia between ex-combatants, victims, and members of communities affected by conflict, Ugarriza and Nussio (2017) find that inter-personal deliberation is conducive to positive intergroup attitudes when small-group discussion protocol emphasizes mutual empathy. Another relevant recent study is by Connors and colleagues (2022), who show that pro-socially motiv-ated participants in small-group discussions arrive at more enlightened and mutually beneficial choices.

My next hypotheses are that **participating in a deliberative minipublic fosters empathy toward those who harbor divergent political opinions (H2) and motivates people to engage in more reflective political reasoning (H3) (Figure 1).**

3 Measurement and Empirical Strategy

3.1 Measuring Reflection

Reflection is a complex construct. Capturing the intrapsychic steps that individ-uals undergo in reflecting is challenging, if not altogether elusive. Therefore, my proxies in this Element constitute an attempt. I use two measures to capture the reflectiveness of individuals' political reasoning.

The first proxy is a psychometric measurement of *deliberation within* (Weinmann 2018), which approximates the definition of reflection adopted in this project. Respondents are asked to self-report on a 7-point scale ("1" meaning "strongly disagree" and "7" meaning "strongly agree") how each of the following five items, *(a) reassessing the biases favoring or opposing different arguments, (b) taking responsibility for making up one's own mind about the topic, after listening to or reading the arguments of others, (c) simulating several opinions about the topic, (d) thinking about the arguments for and against ones' own as well as others' opinions, and (e) evaluating the arguments that speak for and against own as well as others' opinions*, describe the development of their thought processes when forming their political views on an issue. However, like most social science measures, this battery is not devoid of shortcomings. First, it relies on self-reported responses; as such, it may be prone to social desirability bias, errors, and other cognitive biases from respondents (Weinmann 2018, 12–13). Second, the processes underlying reflection may not be conscious, or apparent to the individual.

Therefore, in most of my studies, I use the second proxy – *cognitive complexity of political reasoning* – as an indirect measure of reflection. Cognitive complexity of thinking, a widely used construct by social and political psychologists (Brundidge et al. 2014; Owens and Wedeking 2011; Suedfeld 2010; Tetlock 1983), captures the extent to which people's reasoning is unidimensional or multidimensional and encompasses two core elements of reasoning: differentiation and integration. While *differentiation* captures the degree of differentiation between perspectives, dimensions, or solutions to the issue under consideration, *integration* means integrating these different perspectives into reasoning and decision-making (Tausczik and Pennebaker 2010). Out of these two dimensions, one unidimensional score is created that ranges from the least complex to the most complex. The least complex language refers to an individual's "rel[iance] on rigid, one-dimensional, evaluative rules in interpreting events, and [...] mak-[ing] decisions on the basis of only a few salient items of information," whereas the most complex language denotes a language which "interpret[s] events in multidimensional terms and [...] integrate[s] a variety of evidence in arriving at decisions" (Tetlock et al. 1985, 1228).

I capture the cognitive complexity with an open-ended display question that asks individuals to provide justifications for their position on a given issue after having measured their position on the issue. Short essays that individuals write in response to this open-ended question are used to calculate the cognitive complexity score. While it is possible to use manual coding to capture this score, the current trend favors computerized text analysis. This approach aims to overcome challenges associated with manual coding, such as human biases, the labor-intensive nature of coding, and cost considerations. I use a software package called Linguistic Inquiry and World Count (LIWC) to calculate the cognitive complexity score. The LIWC cognitive complexity calculation works under the assumption that "natural language use provides important clues as to how people process information and interpret it to make sense of their environment" (Tausczik and Pennebaker 2010). The scores generated by LIWC are based on LIWC dictionaries with psychometrically validated groups of words. The package analyzes the written text and categorizes each word into psychologically adequate groups and generates the percentage of words in the text that belong to each identified LIWC category. In calculating the cognitive complexity score, I employ ten LIWC indicators (e.g., causation, insight, certainty) (Owens and Wedeking 2011; Wyss et al. 2015).[9] These indicators are put into a formula to calculate one quantity of interest, *cognitive complexity of thinking score.*

---

[9] See the supplementary materials of Muradova and Arceneaux (2022b) for more detailed information.

3.2 Measurement of Empathy

As mentioned elsewhere, I conceptualize empathy as a multidimensional construct, incorporating both affective (affective empathy) and cognitive (perspective-taking) aspects. Affective empathy encompasses the feelings of warmth and concern felt toward the other, while perspective-taking entails actively imagining the feelings, thoughts, and lives of the other. Furthermore, I'm interested in *situational empathy*, that is, empathy elicited by different situational contexts, as opposed to dispositional empathy, a trait-level stable characteristic (Davis 1983). Finally, the focus is on *empathy for the other side*, conceptualized as empathy toward one's political opponent, someone one disagrees with on a political matter.

For Study 1 (Section 4) I manipulate empathy, while for Studies 2 and 3, I measure it. To measure the affective dimension of situational empathy, where relevant, I use the Emotional Response Questionnaire (McCullough et al. 1997). Respondents are asked to indicate (on an 11-point scale, with "1" meaning *not at all,* and "10" meaning *very much*) the extent to which they felt *sympathetic, empathic, concerned, moved, compassionate, warm, soft-hearted,* and *tender,* when deliberating in a group or reading the text about their political opponent. These items are summed to form an index. To capture the cognitive empathy, I use the items tapping into perspective-taking dimension of the influential Interpersonal Reactivity Index by Davis (1983) and adapt them to capture situational (rather than dispositional) cognitive empathy.

3.3 Research Methods

This Element applies a mixed-method research design (Tashakkori and Teddlie 2021) and brings together both quantitative and qualitative data. H1 is tested with the help of a large survey experiment fielded in the UK (Study 1, Section 4), where empathy is manipulated. To study H2 and H3, I first take an exploratory mode, by relying on a case study of a real-world deliberative institution – the Irish Citizens' Assembly – with the data from participant observation, and in-depth interviews (Study 2, Section 5). I then proceed to a confirmatory mode by studying the relationship between small-group deliberation and reflection (H3) via a quasi-experiment (Belgium) (Study 3, Section 6) and a laboratory experiment (UK) (Study 4, Section 6). I further investigate the scalability of H3 to a larger public, by isolating one element of interpersonal deliberation, *exposure to cross-cutting information,* with a cross-national survey experiment in the UK and Chile (Study 5, Section 6). Table 1 presents the list of empirical studies and descriptive information about them.

Table 1 List of empirical studies that test the theory

Study	Country	Part of the theory	Method	Outcome variable(s)
Study 1: UBI (2019)	UK	(H1)	Survey experiment	Cognitive complexity of reasoning
Study 2: ICA (2017–2018), issues: abortion, climate change, and aging population	Ireland	(H2) and (H3)	Participant observation Interviews	Empathy for the other side Deliberation within
Study 3: Assisted dying (2018–2019)	Belgium	(H2) and (H3)	Pretest-posttest quasi experiment	Empathy for the other side Cognitive complexity of reasoning
Study 4: Assisted dying (2018)	UK	(H3)	Laboratory experiment	Deliberation within
Study 5: UBI (2019, 2020)	UK and Chile	Scaling up H3	Survey experiment	Cognitive complexity of reasoning

4 Study 1: Empathy for the Other Side and Policy Attitudes on Universal Basic Income

My first study examines whether and how empathy for the other side in the context of a political disagreement can influence people's political opinion formation on the issue of universal basic income (hereinafter UBI) in the UK.[10] The objective is to see whether empathy can motivate people to move beyond the dismissal of opposing perspectives on the issue; and actively incorporate these views in their political reasoning. The study is an online survey experiment that induces empathy in individuals for a person holding opposing views on UBI and measures the reflectiveness of their political reasoning posttreatment.

4.1 Issue Context

While UBI is not a single homogeneous policy, its core idea is that everyone should receive a regular, universal, nontaxable, and non-means-tested cash payment from the government to guarantee a minimum standard of living and cover essential needs. The payment amount varies by country and ideology, and its structure depends on the specific scheme. While discussions about UBI trace back to the eighteenth century (see Bidadanure 2019), the policy has recently gained prominence in mainstream political discourse, with countries like Canada, Kenya, Uganda, Finland, and others experimenting with various trial schemes. One contributing factor to this increased interest is concern over labor force automation. When Study 1 was conducted, UBI was a contentious issue in several European countries, including the Netherlands, Finland, and Switzerland. In the UK, public support for UBI was divided but generally leaned toward approval, with approximately 50 percent of Brits in favor according to the European Social Survey (ESS 2016). Around this time, the Scottish government, led by Nicola Sturgeon, expressed interest in implementing pilot UBI experiments in several localities. However, the pilot scheme was ultimately not pursued due to concerns about its impracticality.

4.2 Study Design

This study focuses on how empathy influences individuals' political reasoning in the context of political disagreement. The core expectation is that empathy for one's policy opponent will increase the reflectiveness of people's political reasoning. A survey experiment was conducted in which political disagreement

---

[10] This section is based on a study reported at Muradova and Arceneaux (2022b).

was induced by a text vignette. Individuals were exposed to a short text about a fictitious character – Sarah – who is either in favor or against the UBI, providing a justification for her position. The experiment was designed so that Sarah's position on UBI was always opposite to that of the respondent. The text includes Sarah's photo to enhance realism and engagement. This was held constant across placebo and empathy conditions. Thus, respondents in both conditions were exposed to political disagreement through a text about Sarah and her position on UBI. Empathy for the other was induced via a writing assignment (Todd and Galinsky 2014). Individuals randomly assigned to the empathy condition were instructed to actively imagine the feelings and thoughts of their policy opponent, Sarah, and to write about what they had imagined.

The design also included a control condition in which individuals neither read about Sarah nor received empathy instructions. They only completed a pre- and post-survey. The objective was to account for the effects of time. I summarize the structure of the experiment in Figure 2.

4.3 Sample

We preregistered and conducted a survey experiment in March 2019 with a sample of 2,014 British residents, recruited through the survey company Dynata. The subject pool was non-probability based but nationally representative across census age, gender, and region (see the supplementary materials of Muradova and Arceneaux 2022b for more information).

4.4 Measures

Reflection was measured through the cognitive complexity (CC) of political reasoning, captured using an open-ended display item. After measuring respondents' posttreatment policy attitudes on UBI, individuals were asked to provide written justifications for their position in four to five sentences. Individuals' policy attitudes on UBI were measured using a question from the European Social Survey, which provided a brief overview of a hypothetical UBI scheme. They were then asked to indicate their support or opposition to implementing this scheme in the UK, using a scale from 1 ("strongly oppose") to 6 ("strongly favor"). Using automated text analysis with validated dictionaries, we calculated the cognitive complexity score from the qualitative short essays written by individuals. As stated in the previous section, cognitive complexity taps into the multidimensional reasoning, that is the hallmark of reflection. It captures how individuals define and integrate different dimensions of the issue in their reasoning.

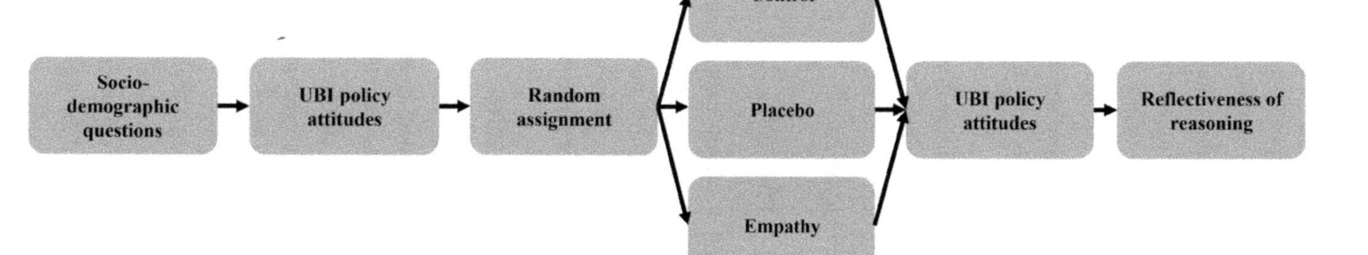

Figure 2 Experimental design.

Note: Individuals in the placebo and empathy conditions encountered political disagreement. Those in the empathy condition were instructed to imagine themselves in the shoes of their policy opponent and write their thoughts. In contrast, the control group completed only pre- and post-questionnaires.

I also measured the extent of affective empathy – feelings of empathic concern – toward the issue opponent whose perspective participants were trying to take. Participants rated their feelings of sympathy, empathy, concern, compassion, warmth, and kindness toward Sarah on a scale of 1 to 5.

Finally, although it is not the primary outcome variable, I examined whether empathy for the other leads to attitude change on UBI by calculating the mean difference between post- and pretreatment attitudes.

4.5 Results

The preexperimental survey shows that the majority of individuals in our sample favor UBI (Figure 3). Approximately 65.3 percent of respondents are either "slightly," "somewhat" or "strongly" in favor of introducing a UBI scheme in the UK. On average, baseline support for UBI differs across gender, age, political ideology, and partisanship. Younger and more liberal individuals are more supportive of UBI, while supporters of the Conservative Party, UKIP, and non-partisans are significantly less so.

First, I begin by exploring the extent to which the empathy treatment induced the feelings of affective empathy in respondents toward their issue opponents, by comparing the mean affective empathy (a sum index of sympathy, empathy, concern, being moved, compassion, warmth, and soft-heartedness; rescaled to 0–1) across placebo and empathy conditions.

Figure 4 shows that individuals in the empathy condition experienced greater affective empathy toward their issue opponent ($M = 0.33$; $SD = 0.24$) than those in

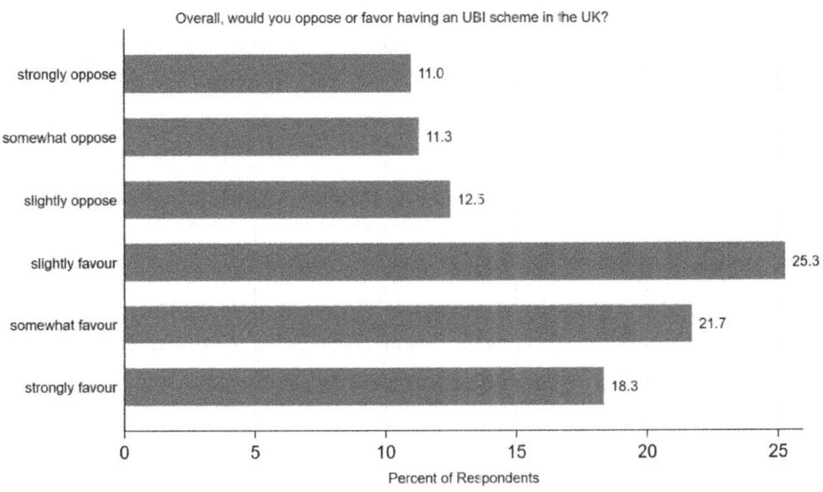

Figure 3 Baseline support for UBI

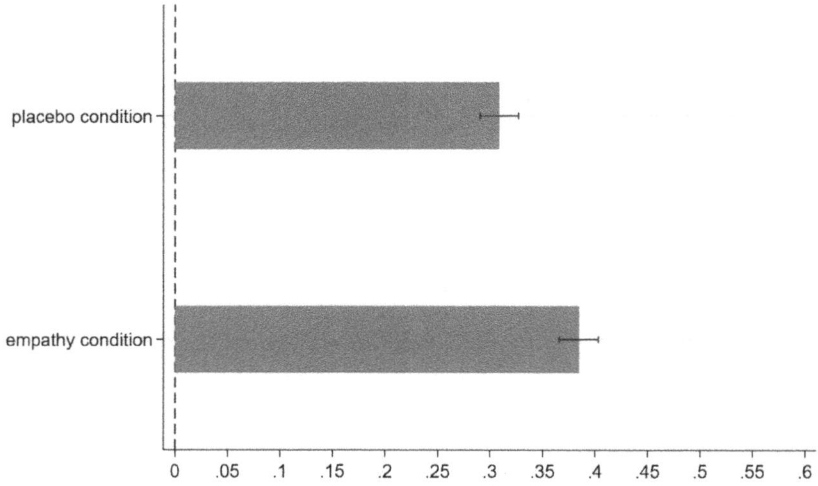

Figure 4 Affective empathy elicited by the writing assignment

the placebo condition (M = 0.31; SD = 0.23). In standardized terms, the effect is equal to one-third of a standard deviation (SD). Our treatment encouraged individuals to feel empathy for their issue opponents despite differing political views.

To test my hypothesis on empathy's impact on the reflectiveness of political reasoning, I estimate its effect on the standardized cognitive complexity score (Model 1, Figure 5), using the placebo condition (political disagreement without empathy instructions) as the baseline. The findings show that imagining life from the perspective of someone with counter-attitudinal views increases the cognitive complexity of people's political reasoning. In other words, upon imagining their issue opponent's thoughts and feelings, respondents began entertaining diverse perspectives and integrating them into their reasoning. The magnitude of the effect equals to 0.13 SD. Empathy for the other side effectively encourages individuals to be more reflective in their political reasoning. Even after controlling for individual characteristics like political partisanship, the positive effect of empathy remains robust (see Muradova and Arceneaux 2022b).

As shown in Table 2, the mean cognitive complexity scores across three conditions reveal that political disagreement alone (vs. control) reduces the reflectiveness of political thinking about UBI. This supports the idea that exposure to opposing views can strengthen prior attitudes and lead to less reflective, more directionally motivated reasoning (Wojcieszak and Price 2010; Guess and Coppock 2020 for a review). However, this observed effect is not statistically significant at conventional levels.

Table 2 Mean (standardized) cognitive complexity score across experimental conditions

Control	0.00	(0.04)
Placebo	−0.04	(0.04)
Empathy	0.09	(0.04)
N		2014

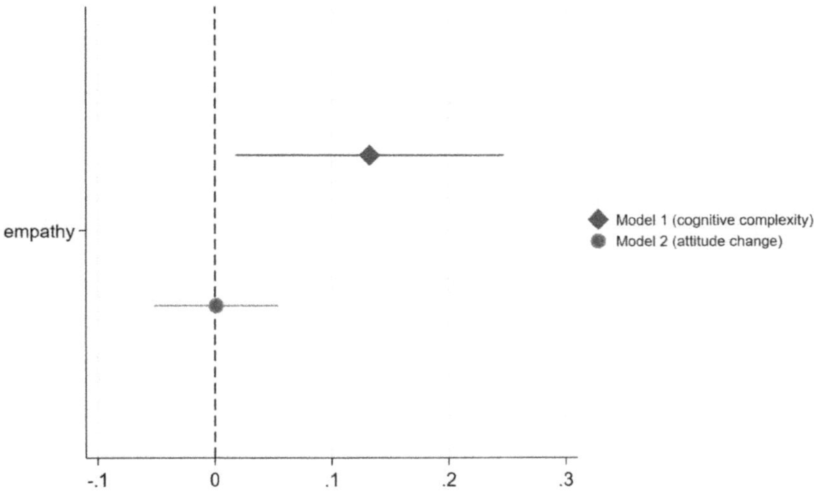

Figure 5 The effect of empathy on reflective political thinking

Finally, I explore whether the effect of empathy translates into significant attitude changes. The OLS regression results (Model 2, Figure 5) show that empathy treatment neither increases nor decreases individuals' likelihood of shifting their attitudes on UBI. While their political reasoning becomes more reflective, it doesn't translate into mean attitude change, at least in the short term.

4.6 Discussion

This study finds that when individuals are motivated to empathize with their policy opponents, they become more open to considering diverse and opposing perspectives. Even amid political disagreement, empathy for those with opposing views to ours can foster more reflective political thinking. The effect size of empathy on reflection is consistent with the effect sizes observed in real-world interventions designed to change people's attitudes (e.g., Kalla and Broockman 2023).

5 Study 2: Political Institutions that Elicit Empathy for the Other Side – The Irish Citizens' Assembly (2016–2018)

There were elderly people, who would have been raised in a very Catholic environment […], they were totally opposed to abortion. They made it totally clear from day one that they had huge issues with this. Towards the end [of discussions], they would say: 'that is still how all stands, that is how I feel … But I totally understand why things need to change for *other* people […]. I will not vote […] [my] way, even though this goes against my beliefs'. I thought it was empathetic, brave, and unselfish. I could see these people were really struggling; that was the core of their belief; that was how they grew up; that was ingrained [in them], you know. Yet, they decided that changes need to happen, even though [they] did not believe in it. […] a very hard decision for many people … not just some sort of a throw-away decision, […] there was a lot of soul-searching for a lot of people.
(An interviewee, male, in his late 30s, a member of the ICA, talking about the Irish Citizens' Assembly processes on legalizing abortion in Ireland)

In the booth, the ballot booth, when I was voting, after all the information we had heard … from the witnesses especially […], when I stood in that voting booth and a woman stood in front of me, and I said, 'I cannot make a decision for you'. I would have had views that said, 'Yes, but under these circumstances, and yes, under those' … then I found myself … I would still find myself in the conservative end [of the issue] […]. But I said, I am not going to be the one to say, […] 'You cannot have it.' …
(An interviewee, female, in her early 50s, a member of the ICA, talking about the Irish Citizens' Assembly processes on legalizing abortion in Ireland)

To understand the potential of a deliberative institution to elicit empathy for the other side, I conduct an in-depth case study of a real-world deliberative institution, the Irish Citizens' Assembly (2016–2018) (hereinafter ICA). In doing so, I rely on data from extensive participant observation, and in-depth interviews with the members of the ICA.

5.1 Description of the ICA

The ICA brought together a cross-section of the Irish public to learn from expert evidence and witnesses, engage with each other, consider several contentious socio-political issues concerning Irish society, and make informed recommendations. On its official website, the ICA is defined as "an exercise in deliberative democracy, giving voice to citizens and placing them at the heart of important legal and policy issues facing Irish society" (https://citizensassembly.ie).

The ICA was initiated by the Irish Government, approved by both Houses of the Irish Oireachtas (Parliament) in 2016, and operated until 2018. It was tasked with considering five high-priority socio-political issues: legalizing abortion, responding to the challenges and opportunities of an aging population, fixed-term parliaments, the manner in which referenda are held, and tackling climate change. The primary objective of convening the ICA, however, was to address the contentious and partisan constitutional issue of legalizing abortion, known as "repeal of the 8th amendment".[11] Commentators argue that the constitution and approval of the ICA on abortion were driven by pressure from abortion activists and civil society organizations (see, e.g., O'Shaughnessy 2022). This pressure compelled the newly elected minority government, led by Enda Kenny, the leader of the liberal-conservative and Christian-democratic party, Fine Gael, to act.

The ICA consisted of ninety-nine Irish citizens (plus one independent chair), chosen through citizen lottery, and broadly representative of the Irish population along sociodemographic variables such as age, sex, region, and socioeconomic group.[12] The stratified random system for the recruitment of members ensured that the spectrum of opinions, perspectives and voices broadly mirrored that of the wider Irish society. Activists and lobbyists were explicitly excluded from the recruitment process. The members received remuneration for their travel expenses and were provided with accommodation during the weekends of deliberations.

The sessions of the ICA comprised the following parts. First, prior to deliberations, citizens were provided with written information about the topic, which included printed expert presentations and a summary of the submitted suggestions and viewpoints from the larger public.[13] Second, participants were presented with evidence from both national and international experts offering diverse perspectives, along with firsthand accounts from individuals with lived experiences related to the topic under discussion. Third, they engaged in facilitated small-group deliberations with different others. The length of deliberations varied by issue, ranging from five weekends (abortion) to one weekend (referenda). The deliberations ultimately culminated in voting on one or several specific recommendations. Voting was conducted via secret ballot and overseen

---

[11] The 8th amendment to the Irish constitution, approved in 1983, guaranteed the right to life of the unborn, making abortion constitutionally illegal except in cases where there was a life-threatening risk to the mother. The ICA and subsequent referendum aimed to determine whether the 8th Amendment should be repealed.

[12] Stratified random sampling was used to recruit the subjects. A market research company, RED C, was responsible for cold calling door-to-door to recruit ninety-nine subjects and an additional ninety-nine substitute members (see Farrell et al. 2023).

[13] Submissions played a key role in the ICA process. The general public had the opportunity to share their views on the issue by submitting their perspectives and suggestions, which enriched the debate. All submissions were published on the ICA website (https://citizensassembly.ie/submissions/).

by the independent chair, along with the participation of two other assembly members. The results of the vote were submitted to the Irish Parliament for further deliberation and policy action.

5.2 Case Selection

The choice of the ICA for this case study is driven by the following reasons. First, the ICA exemplifies a deliberative institution, with a design that incorporates essential institutional features of a normatively desirable deliberative process. Additionally, the ICA is a real-world institution with clearly defined ties to the larger democratic political decision-making processes in Ireland. Since 2013, citizens' assemblies have become an integral part of political decision-making in Ireland. Ireland started this tradition with the Constitutional Convention (2013–2014),[14] followed by the ICA (2016–2018), Citizens' Assembly on Gender Equality (2020–2021), Dublin Citizens' Assembly (2022), Citizens' Assembly on Biodiversity Loss (2022), and Citizens' Assembly on Drugs Use (2023) (www.citizensassembly.ie).

The recommendations from the citizens' assemblies have wielded significant influence over Irish policy-making. Since the advent of the first Irish deliberative minipublic, six referendums were approved and took place, stemming from the recommendations by these assemblies. These referendums resulted in historic constitutional changes on abortion, same-sex marriage, and blasphemy. Similarly, the ICA recommendations on climate change found their way into the Irish Government's Climate Action Plan of June 2019. While not all the recommendations were embraced, the plan incorporated several ambitious proposals, including a substantial rise in the carbon tax from 20 to 80 euros per ton and a notable increase in the proportion of renewables in the energy mix, targeting a shift from 30 to 70 percent before the year 2030. The assembly on biodiversity loss recommended a future referendum on the constitutional amendment concerning biodiversity sometime in the future. A referendum will determine whether the Irish constitution should be amended to bestow environmental rights upon nature. Lastly, on the 8th of March 2024, consistent with the recommendations of the citizens' assembly on gender equality, two constitutional referendums concerning the concepts of family and care in the Irish constitution, took place in Ireland. Both suggested amendments were rejected by an overwhelming majority of the Irish voters.

---

[14] The convention on the constitution was convened by the Irish government and considered a set of issues, including same-sex marriage and blasphemy. The convention consisted of 66 randomly chosen lay citizens, and 29 members of the parliament. This made it different from the subsequent citizens' assemblies whose members were lay people only.

The ICA (2016–2018) garnered significant media attention, particularly for its deliberations on the complex and contentious issue of liberalizing abortion law. The ICA deliberations on abortion happened "under the glare of publicity" (Farrell et al. 2023, 55). After five weekends of deliberation (November 2016 to April 2017), the ICA's recommendations were submitted to a special Oireachtas committee. Following further discussions by elected politicians, the committee recommended and called for a referendum in summer of 2018.

The ICA vote results showed overwhelming support from members to replace the constitutional article with a new provision decriminalizing and legalizing abortion and providing abortion on request. Notably, this support was achieved despite a nontrivial number of participants who initially held either conservative views or were undecided prior to the deliberative process. The abortion referendum, with a near-record turnout of 64 percent, resulted in the removal of the abortion ban. Observers noted that in addition to directly influencing the call for a referendum and the wording of the referendum question, the ICA views and recommendations were eventually reflected in the referendum vote of the Irish voters (Farrell et al. 2023). Sixty-six percent of the electorate voted to repeal the 8th Amendment, closely matching the 64 percent vote from the ICA members.

5.3 The ICA and Empathy

The ICA members were provided with dedicated time and resources to engage in in-depth discussions and carefully consider the policy issues under discussion. These deliberations took place in a setting that functioned like a mediated intergroup environment. The question driving this section is: Which institutional features of the ICA fostered empathic perspective-taking and reflection? To answer this question, I draw on extensive participant observation (Kawulich 2005) and semi-structured, in-depth interviews with eleven ICA members to gain insights into the process.

Between September 2017 and February 2018, I closely observed the ICA sessions. It was essential for me to be physically present, acquaint myself with the ICA, and directly observe the processes shaping the assembly meetings. I took notes of my observations, documented, and interpreted them to understand the process better. I paid special attention to the behaviors and verbal and nonverbal expressions of participating individuals. The observation extended to spaces beyond the formal venues of the assembly, including the hotel lobby, corridors, and restrooms. I complemented my observation with informal talks with the members of the organizing committee and the experts who were part of the process. The goal was to understand the process, discover fresh insights, and identify recurring patterns in the expressions and behaviors of participating individuals. Additionally, I conducted in-depth semi-structured interviews with eleven members of the ICA (four females and seven males).[15] Consistent with Saunders et al. (2018), I used data saturation as a criterion for discontinuing interviews.

In the subsequent portion of this section, I outline the main recurring patterns derived from both interview data and my participant observation. First, the ICA fostered an environment wherein individuals cultivated emotional bonds, surfaced, and flourished both in formal and informal spaces of the ICA. In addition to being a formal deliberating event bringing together a diverse group of people to consider complex socio-political issues, the ICA was first and foremost a social event that engaged people's emotions. Emotional engagement served as the initial catalyst for members' cognitive involvement with the information and with different perspectives. Despite long and hard discussions on divisive topics, like abortion and climate change, participating individuals managed to forge friendships across profound political divides.

> The process is so engaging, [...], that you meet people, friends as well, [...].
> One of them [became] a very good friend of mine. I got to meet her on the
> fourth day. We sat there, cracking jokes [...] that broke the ice. [...] It is
> especially the social end of things. To hear what other people are doing in their
> lives, the similarities, you know ... (male, in his 50s)

As illustrated by the following two quotes, the social aspects of the ICA meetings were crucial for getting to know different others and understand where they were coming from. Social bonding facilitated the formation of shared hopes and goals.

> [W]hen the meetings are over, you are going to your dinner, and discuss
> something else, sport or whatever .... Discuss families [...] It is like
> bonding. People feel like they are a part of something. (male, in his late 40s)

> [I]f you are going to talk about such difficult things [...], such intense kind
> of discussions, it is important to be able to have a bit of laugh, a bit of
> comradery with people. [...] Especially, when we are seeing each other all
> the time. [...] It is nice to have a bit of laugh with people. [...] It enlightens
> the mood. (female, in her 20s)

Emotional engagement, nurtured within a safe, inclusive, and respectful setting, laid the groundwork for frank conversations.

> [T]he most important thing [...] is people being respectful. It is just respect
> for those different views, that variety of opinions; and I have not come across

---

[15] See Muradova (2020) for more information.

anybody that has been outright disrespectful of other people's opinions. You can sit back, listen, and then make your point, knowing that you do not agree or whatever. But there has never been any kind of backlash, if you will, for having an opinion that was not the popular opinion at the table […]. Everybody feels like it is a safe space for their opinion, even if they know that it is not going to be popular with the people at the table. (female, in her 20s)

[T]he set-up of the whole thing […]. The secretariat set it up in a way that it makes it easy to talk. There is no fear. You feel confident talking and expressing opinions and knowing that [no-one] will take an offense or will get upset about. I think that the fact that we get information from both sides, and as I see, non-confrontational manner, so the information given is to use to listen, to digest and reflect upon, and then vote upon it at various stages. (male, in his late 40s)

I felt very free to express my view without fear of being denigrated or of being made feel small; it does not matter what point of view you have to make … to feel free to make it [is what counts]. (female, in her early 50s)

Through its design, ICA created three conditions that promoted empathy for the opposing side. First, it actively motivated empathic engagement. The organizers consistently encouraged members to stay open to each other's arguments, perspectives, and life experiences. The ICA was governed with six key principles: openness (including openness to hear from all other members of the wider society via submissions), fairness (diverse perspectives on every issue to be heard during deliberations along with the provision of high-quality briefing materials), equality of voice (everyone has the right to express their views), efficiency (good time management), and respect and collegiality. These principles were consistently reinforced in each session, actively encouraged, and nurtured throughout the meetings.

Second, the presence of diverse opinions and perspectives at the ICA enabled participants to imagine what the others' lives looked like, and why they held the perspectives that they held. Diversity was ensured at different stages during the ICA processes. First, the topics discussed impacted various segments of Irish society. Abortion clearly affected the women. Climate change pertained mostly to the future generations, while the aging population concerned the elderly. Second, the ICA tried to resemble a microcosm of the Irish society, at least with regards to age, education, gender, and region, as well as the baseline perspectives they held at the start of the process. Third, one of the characteristics of the ICA meetings was that the members of each small group would be rotated at every meeting. The aim was to ensure participants didn't sit with the same people, but instead were exposed to a diverse range of individuals and perspectives. One interviewee, referencing deliberations on Ireland's aging population, stated:

> [A] lot of the kind of personal stuff were self-generated, within the people who had already experienced that, you know, dealing with elderly relatives. […] Let us not to forget, because of the population spread within the group, there was, you know, the number of elderly, yeah, so they […] had an opinion, because a lot directly affects them. […] For people who are little bit younger to have one to one conversation, that, or round table conversation, was important. (male, in his late 30s)

Third, the ICA, via its design, created and continuously nurtured an environment where all kinds of arguments were welcomed – both fact-based, rational information and more emotional expressions, such as personal stories, narratives, testimonies, and humor. In addition to the statistical and factual evidence presented by experts, the ICA invited witnesses to share their lived experiences. For example, on the issue of abortion, members heard from women directly impacted by Ireland's abortion ban, including rape survivors who had to travel abroad for the procedure. They also heard from doctors who performed abortions and organizations supporting vulnerable women from disadvantaged backgrounds. On the issue of climate change, nonexpert speakers shared their personal experiences in proactively dealing with its challenges. One speaker had founded a nonprofit that connected supermarkets with impoverished citizens, aiming to contribute to tackling both food waste and hunger.

Stories and narratives helped members navigate complex issues. Everyday language on climate change, especially from nonexpert witnesses, encouraged individuals to see it as an issue impacting daily life, fostering a deeper, more personal connection (Muradova et al. 2020). Personal stories and narratives were especially powerful on moral issues like abortion and elderly care. Consider the following thoughts from one interviewee:

> [O]ther people's experiences … sometimes we sit in these sessions … we may not fully realize that individual experiences at the end of the day is actually big experiences, you know, you are talking about things that affect people's lives, and quite often can change their lives. (female, in her late 50s)

For another member, the interplay between factual evidence and personal stories was crucial to the deliberative process of abortion:

> [T]he first few meetings were specifically about facts, and statistics. […] They [referring to the organizers] wanted to make sure that we understood the facts surrounding the 8th amendment, around the constitution, around what currently is happening. […] Further along the process, because some of it was kind of abstract, then became more personal, when we heard personal

> stories of some of the women involved. We heard the recordings of them. We heard from advocacy groups, stuff like this. So that brought personal, more emotive part from a late date once we had a grounding in proper factual information. (male, in his late 30s)

Personal stories enhanced individuals' empathic understanding and concern for others. This is illustrated by a quote from a young female member discussing the issues surrounding the aging population.

> Personal stories ... it is the part that gets you in the guts. It is the part you actually feel something ... hearing that it is somebody's story. We heard one story of an older lady who had been put in a care home, against her will basically, and you know that was just incredibly sad, no amount of statistics could give you what actually happens on the ground, what actually happens in people's lives. Because you cannot boil down the people to numbers, generally speaking. (female, in her 20s)

Stories and testimonies brought out compassion and understanding among the members. Consider the following quotes regarding the deliberations on legalizing abortion.

> [T]hey had people speak via tape recorder about their experience on the termination [of pregnancy] [...], and there were six people. [...] and it was very powerful. You can never [...] ignore the lived experience." (female, in her late 50s)

> "[I]f you take something like the 8th amendment, listening to conversation of women who already experienced. Their experiences, good or bad, kind of gives you greater insight of what it is like to walk in that person's shoes. [...] that has emotional impact on how you would vote on the issue. (male, in his early 40s)

An overwhelming majority of the interviewees reported that their experience at the ICA made them much more empathetic overall, beyond the confines of the assembly meetings. This can be best illustrated by the following quotes.

> [W]hen I am in a discussion in a pub and outside of this, I would be a lot more tolerant listening to somebody state something that I disagree with. I would be more ... I would be looking for more follow-up ... A little more, a kind of understanding. (male, in his late 30s)

> I'd be a lot of more patient in the face of the opinions that do not necessarily align themselves with my own. I think, I would be a little bit, [...] more respectful and patient with, you know, diverging opinions, than previously. That is probably been my, personally my biggest takeaway. [...]I would now have more than of an ability to do that. In the first meeting, if somebody

> disagreed with me, I would be little bit more like, 'how can you think that,
> you know, how can you think that?' Now, I would be like … 'Ok, I do not
> agree with you, but ok' … I would have more difficult discussions [now].
> (female, in her 20s)

> Before I would have … been probably under the basis of if somebody had
> a conflicting view to me, I would go, yea, idiot … Now I'm more open-
> minded. I have seen people, people that were presenting to us and also fellow
> citizens who have conflicting views. Everybody is entitled to those views. My
> views might, to somebody else, look idiotic or strange. I realize it now. When
> I see people, hear people, I kind of go, well, these are your views, you [may]
> not know all the facts, fair enough. (male, in his early 30s)

In sum, the institutional characteristics of the ICA motivated and facilitated the processes of empathy for the other side. Affective engagement of the members of the ICA was a necessary condition for empathy to be evoked in interpersonal deliberative settings. Despite its central focus on learning and deliberating, human emotions and social bonding took a central stage in these processes. Sharing a friendly and respectful space over an extended period allowed distant individuals to get to know each other, connect with one another's lives, and bond, resulting in greater emotional responsiveness to each other's perspectives despite political differences on contentious issues. Emotionally engaged individuals were more inclined to empathize with the other side. Furthermore, two institutional characteristics of the assembly were crucial in facilitating the processes of empathy for the other side: the presence of diversity of perspectives, and the interplay of fact-based rational argumentation and storytelling and narratives during deliberations.

5.4 The ICA and Reflection

My data from the ICA also shows that reflection does not necessarily or always lead to a significant shift in attitudes and positions. Past research on the ICA and other assemblies indicated that participation in such institutions can result in noticeable attitudinal changes. For instance, Farrell and colleagues (2023) show that on the issue of abortion, participating at ICA led to significant opinion transformation toward more liberal positions, in particular, among those who were undecided. However, the outcome of reflective thinking is not always an attitude change. Reflection can lead to other equally, if not more, crucial nuanced outcomes that are difficult to capture through survey data.

During the interviews, some members noted that although they maintained their pre-deliberation positions (e.g., on legalizing abortion or climate change), their attitudes underwent a transformation: they became more informed about the issues, resulting in stronger positions after discussions and reflection. The following quotes are good illustrations of this reasoning:

> I'd say that I stayed pro-choice, but I did swing. I was pro-choice. I was not a fanatical pro-choice, just pro-choice. It was, then, given all the information ... Then, I heard the arguments from the pro-life side, and then I was ... 'they have a point, they have a point, but I still see the reason of having the choice'. So, I would have been less pro-choice than I was, but I am still pro-choice. (male, in his early 60s)

> [M]y opinion on these topics did not change massively. [...] It evolved a little bit [...]. The most I probably learned was from climate change. I did not really have an opinion on it, other than I knew [that] the climate change [was] a problem. I wouldn't have had any particular opinion on the thing that needs to be done. [...] I have learned most on that one. (female, in her 20s)

Contrary psychological processes also emerged. For some, participation at the ICA led to the moderation of their conservative views on the issue of abortion:

> I would have had a view, but having heard the information that we were given, my view has softened. I would not say that my view changed radically, but it became less conservative. [...] I am not in a position to stand in a position of judging anybody else in terms of changing the legislation, changing the constitution. (female, in her early 50s)

Perhaps the most surprising finding of this study was that empathy led some individuals to vote against their deeply entrenched beliefs on the morally divisive issue of abortion. This perfectly illustrates how reflection can change political behavior without first altering beliefs and attitudes. Two quotes at the outset of this section illustrate this idea. Repeating one such quote:

> In the booth, the ballot booth, when I was voting, after all the information we had heard ... from the witnesses especially [...], when I stood in that voting booth and a woman stood in front of me, and I said, 'I cannot make a decision for you'. I would have had views that said, 'Yes, but under these circumstances, and yes, under those' ... then I found myself ... I would still find myself in the conservative end [of the issue] [...] But I said, I am not going to be the one to say [...]: 'You cannot have it' ... (female, in her early 50s)

5.5 The ICA and Partisan Politics

This Element focuses on the microlevel psychological processes underlying interpersonal deliberation at the ICA. However, understanding the broader political landscape surrounding the ICA's establishment is crucial, as it may have played a role in influencing the behavior of the ICA members during and beyond the deliberative process. For example, one might ponder the role of conventional partisan politics in these processes, questioning whether the ICA created a nonpartisan environment, and how dynamics within the ICA might unfold differently in more partisan contexts.

Deliberations of the ICA did not happen in a vacuum and were not divorced from conventional partisan politics. First, the ICA's predecessor, the Constitutional Convention, was established by the coalition government formed after the 2011 election, comprising Fine Gael (a liberal-conservative and Christian-democratic party) and Labor (a center-left social-democratic party). The ICA was established in accordance with the program led by a Fine Gael – independent minority government. The most recent assemblies were convened under a coalition government of Fianna Fáil (a conservative, Christian-democratic party), Fine Gael and the Green Party. Hence, it would be inaccurate to characterize the ICA as an experiment conducted solely by left-wing politicians. Second, well before the assembly members were recruited and the sessions began, the ICA attracted significant media attention, primarily due to the contentious and partisan nature of its initial agenda: the legalization of abortion. The organization's formation was sometimes seen as a sign that Irish politicians were either unable or unwilling to address this sensitive issue on their own, prompting them to delegate decision-making responsibility to ordinary citizens (Marlborough 2016). The initiative also faced intense scrutiny from both pro-choice and pro-life advocates, each with distinct perspectives. Pro-choice activists called for an immediate referendum on the issue, while pro-life proponents claimed the ICA was inherently biased, and that its outcome was predetermined. Even during the deliberations, pro-life activists voiced their dissent both online and outside the hotel where the discussions were held. Thus, the ICA emerged within a highly charged partisan context.

Deliberations on abortion happened against the backdrop of a polarized political context. However, what the ICA achieved was to help transcend the partisan divide on the issue of legalizing abortion. My qualitative data shows that the ICA created and nurtured a safe and neutral space, where individuals were encouraged to set aside their ideology, partisanship, and their preconceived ideas about the issue. The institutional characteristics of the ICA that elicited empathy in individuals helped individuals to transcend their partisan attachments and prior beliefs and engage in more reflective political thinking and vote accordingly.

5.6 Discussion and Limitations

In this section, I show how a deliberative institution like the Irish Citizens' Assembly (2016–2018) can elicit empathy for the other side among participating individuals, which, in turn, is consequential for their willingness to engage in reflective thinking. My qualitative data showed that institutional characteristics of the ICA enabled and nurtured a safe space where a diversity of perspectives on moral (abortion) and nonmoral (climate change) issues were respected and communicated through diverse communicative tools. The environment engaged people's emotions and led to empathy for different others. Empathy served as a precursor for overcoming preconceived ideas and biases and for engaging in more reflective political reasoning.

However, this study is not without its shortcomings. The first concerns the representativeness of the case study. I rely on a single case, which serves as one example of a larger population of cases. Generalizing the results from a single deliberative institution presents certain challenges. Therefore, future research should explore these questions in different countries and institutional contexts. The second issue concerns the potential self-selection bias in participating in deliberative minipublics. It is possible that members of the ICA, those who chose to participate in this institution, may systematically differ from the broader Irish population (see Jacquet 2017). However, I currently lack the data needed to evaluate the validity of this assumption. What is known about this case is that, even on the sensitive issue of abortion, the ICA brought together individuals with diverse beliefs and attitudes. As part of the process, researchers were not allowed to measure the members' baseline views on abortion before they started their small-group deliberations. Farrell et al. (2023) conducted a survey at the beginning of the third deliberative weekend, which was midway through the deliberation process. This survey included a question regarding the members' stance on legalizing abortion. By this point, members may have already shifted their views after two weekends of deliberation over the span of two months. Nevertheless, the data from Farrell et al. (2023) provides valuable insights into the members' positions at this stage of the process. Their findings indicate that around 41 percent of ICA members remained undecided about the liberalization of abortion, while 5 percent were completely opposed, and the remaining members held liberal positions on the issue. We do not know what proportion of the "undecided" members initially held conservative views versus liberal ones when the deliberation process began. Thus, although the overall composition of the ICA was skewed toward members who already held more liberal positions on abortion, the presence of individuals with opposing perspectives demonstrates that a range of viewpoints was represented in the deliberation. Future research should systematically investigate this question by examining the individual characteristics of those who willingly participated in the process and those who chose not to, focusing particularly on dispositional traits such as empathy and open-minded thinking.

6 Studies 3 to 5: Interpersonal Deliberation and Reflection – Evidence from Experimental Studies

In Section 5, I examined the real-world and influential deliberative forum – the Irish Citizens' Assembly – to demonstrate that, under the right conditions, a deliberative institution can foster empathy and encourage more reflective reasoning among individuals. However, what Section 5 lacks is empirical evidence establishing a causal relationship between small-group interpersonal deliberation and increased reflection. To address this gap, this section presents the findings from three experiments designed to investigate the effect of interpersonal deliberation on reflection.

6.1 Three Experiments

Study 3 (Belgium) and Study 4 (UK) involve small-group discussions about legalizing assisted dying, one of the contested moral questions of our times. The term "assisted dying" typically refers to both physician-assisted suicide (i.e., doctors *prescribing* a life-ending medication at a voluntary request of a seriously ill, but mentally competent patient with an objective of relieving their suffering) and euthanasia (i.e., *administering* a life-ending medication at a voluntary request of a seriously ill, but mentally competent patient with an objective of relieving their suffering). Public interest and support for legalizing assisted dying in western democracies have grown substantively over the years. According to European Social Survey, the majority of surveyed individuals in twelve European countries (69 percent of individuals in the UK and 86 percent in Belgium)[16] believed that euthanasia can be justified (Bottoni 2023). At the time of fielding my experiments (2018/2019), assisted dying was only legal, under specific legal conditions, in Belgium, Canada, Colombia, Luxembourg, the Netherlands, Switzerland, Victoria of Australia, and several US states.[17]

Study 5 (Chile and UK) examines the upscaling effects of interpersonal deliberation, by isolating and causally studying the effect of one important feature of small-group deliberation – exposure to cross-cutting views – on the reflectiveness of people's political judgments. I use a survey experiment to study this relationship in the context of the universal basic income.

---

[16] The question was measured with a scale that ranges from 0 (never justified) to 10 (always justified). These percentages were calculated by grouping the responses from 6 to 10. Those who reported "10" constituted 32 percent of the surveyed Belgian and 21 percent of the surveyed UK citizens.

[17] As of today, assisted dying is also legal in all six states of Australia (since 2022), New Zealand (since 2021), Portugal (since 2023) and Spain (since 2021).

6.2 Study 3: A Quasi-Experiment in Belgium

Design: Study 3 was a pretest-posttest quasi-experiment conducted in Belgium that involved moderated face-to-face discussions in heterogeneous small groups (Figure 6). While it is difficult to satisfy all deliberative ideals in designing small-group deliberation approximating real-world deliberative institutions, the experiment met the following core design conditions. First, subjects were exposed to cross-cutting views on the issue. Everyone received balanced information on the issue of assisted dying. They were invited to read a one-page printed article about legalizing assisted dying, which presented the most common arguments in favor of and against the policy. Moreover, I ensured that each small group was heterogeneous in terms of gender, age, and policy positions. Second, discussions were moderated to ensure that all participants had equal opportunities for discursive engagement. Third, the deliberators collaboratively established rules to ensure respectful group discussions. Lastly, respondents were encouraged to share their perspectives and arguments using a variety of communicative tools, including fact-based arguments, personal stories, and narratives.

Twelve small groups were formed, with an average of six participants in each group (ranging from three to nine).

Sample: Participants were university students, recruited via the international center of a Belgian university. They had diverse educational (e.g., mathematics, humanities, biology, and economics) and country of origin backgrounds (e.g., Turkey, India, Greece, South Africa, and Zimbabwe).[18] The rationale for opting for international (as opposed to local) students was to assure variance and diversity in baseline issue attitudes.

Ninety-five respondents took part in the Wave 1 (November 2018 to February 2019), where I measured individuals' baseline positions on legalizing assisted dying, together with their socio-demographic characteristics ($M_{age} = 26.3$; $SD_{age} = 5.8$; range: 18–47; 65 percent self-identified as female). In Wave 2, respondents were invited to participate in small-group discussions. Seventy-four

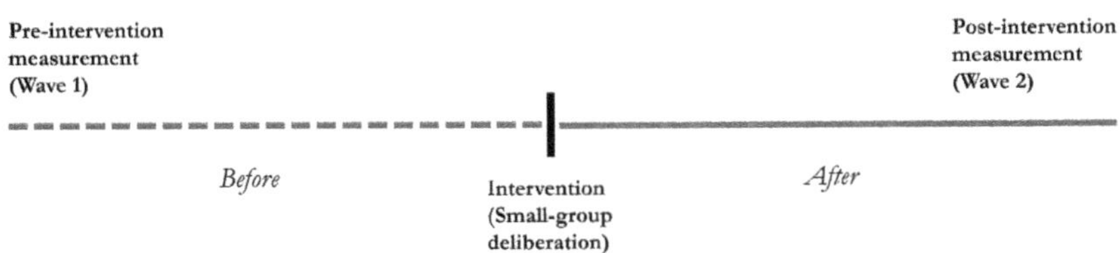

Figure 6 Pretest–posttest experimental design

---

[18] In total, there were thirty-seven nationalities in our sample.

participants took part (M_{age} = 26.6; SD_{age} = 6.4; range: 18–47; 63 percent self-identified as female[19]).

Measures: The main outcome variable of interest, *reflection*, was captured with *cognitive complexity of political reasoning*. The variable was a within-subject change in cognitive complexity (CC) score. The CC was captured with an open-ended question. At Wave 1, individuals were first questioned about their position on legalizing assisted dying. They were asked to indicate, on a scale from 0 to 10, whether they disapproved or approved of legalizing assisted dying in their country of origin (M = 6.9; SD = 3.1, range: 0–10), preceded by a short explanation of what assisted dying entails. Furthermore, participants were given the opportunity to justify their position in four to five sentences through an open-ended question. This question was repeated after the small-group deliberation, allowing for a comparison of responses pre- and posttreatment. The qualitative responses (short essays) were analyzed quantitatively to assess the complexity of their political reasoning. The complexity score was standardized for easier interpretation.

I also measured the level of situational empathy experienced by individuals as a result of small-group deliberation. Both affective and cognitive dimensions of empathy were captured. As a part of the post-deliberation questionnaire, individuals were instructed to indicate, on a 7-point scale, the extent to which they experienced empathic feelings, captured with seven empathy adjectives, including, "compassionate," "warm," "empathic," among others (McCullough et al. 1997). Moreover, situational perspective-taking was measured with four statements from an adapted version of Davis (1983): *(a) I tried to imagine how I would feel if I were in the place of people who thought differently than me, (b) I believe there are at least two sides to the issue of legalizing assisted dying and I tried to look at them both during the discussion, (c) I found it difficult to see things from the other person's point of view, during the discussion (inverse), and (d) One should try to place oneself in the position of the person who thinks differently on the issue of legalization of assisted dying.* Two indices were created and were further rescaled (0–1).

Results: To test whether interpersonal deliberation induces more reflective political reasoning in individuals, I examine within-subject change in cognitive complexity by running paired t-tests comparing (standardized) pre- and post-cognitive complexity scores (Table 3). The results show that respondents' mean cognitive complexity score increased post-discussions (M_{pre} = 0.04; SD_{pre} = 0.96; M_{post} = 0.47, SD_{post} = 0.53, two-tailed $p < 0.00$). The effect is large and substantive, equaling to nearly half a standard deviation (0.43 SD). Engaging in small-group

---

[19] The drop-out rate was primarily due to individuals leaving Belgium at the end of their exchange programs or because the proposed dates and times for the group discussions did not fit their schedules. Post-hoc analyses indicate that dropout was not systematic with respect to socio-demographic factors or attitudes toward legalizing assisted dying.

Table 3 Effect of small-group deliberation

	Mean	**SD**	**Range**
Pretreatment CC score	0.04	0.95	−4.23 to 2.49
Posttreatment CC score	0.47	0.53	−0.71 to 2.18

discussions with diverse participants on the issue of legalizing assisted dying enhanced the reflectiveness of the participants' political reasoning.[20]

We proceed to examine the distribution of affective and cognitive empathy that individuals experienced as a result of small-group deliberation. Our design lacks both a control condition and a pretreatment measure for situational empathy. Therefore, the results reported here are descriptive, rather than causal. Figure 7 shows that the distribution of empathy in both cases is skewed to the right. On a scale from 0 to 1, the mean situational cognitive empathy is $M = 0.62$ (SD = 0.26), a bit more than the experienced affective empathy ($M = 0.55$, SD = 0.22). The majority of respondents indicated that they tended to empathize with those who held opposing views on the issue and experienced feelings of empathic concern during small-group deliberation.

6.3 Study 4: A Laboratory Experiment in the UK

Design: The subsequent study is a laboratory experiment conducted in a mid-sized university city in the UK. The primary treatment involves small-group deliberation on the issue of legalizing assisted dying. Similar to Study 3, this study also consists of two waves. A larger pool of subjects was recruited during the first stage. In Wave 2, participants were randomly assigned to one of three experimental conditions – control group, information group, or deliberation group – using the Z-tree program. The washout period between Wave 1 and Wave 2 ranged from 8 to 23 days (see Figure 8).

Those who were randomly assigned to the information group were invited to the lab to complete a survey. After reading the instructions and signing the informed consent form, participants took a short survey. Initially, they were asked to read an article about legalizing assisted dying in the UK, which presented four arguments in favor and four against the policy, commonly

---

[20] Although it is not the primary focus of my studies, I also examined potential attitude changes regarding the legalization of assisted dying following the discussions. The results of a paired *t*-test comparing pre- and post-discussion attitudes among participants in both Wave 1 and Wave 2 revealed no statistically significant within-subject attitude transformation ($M_{pre} = 7$, $SD_{pre} = 3.05$; $M_{post} = 7.07$, $SD_{post} = 3.26$; range: 0–10; two-tailed $p < 0.78$).

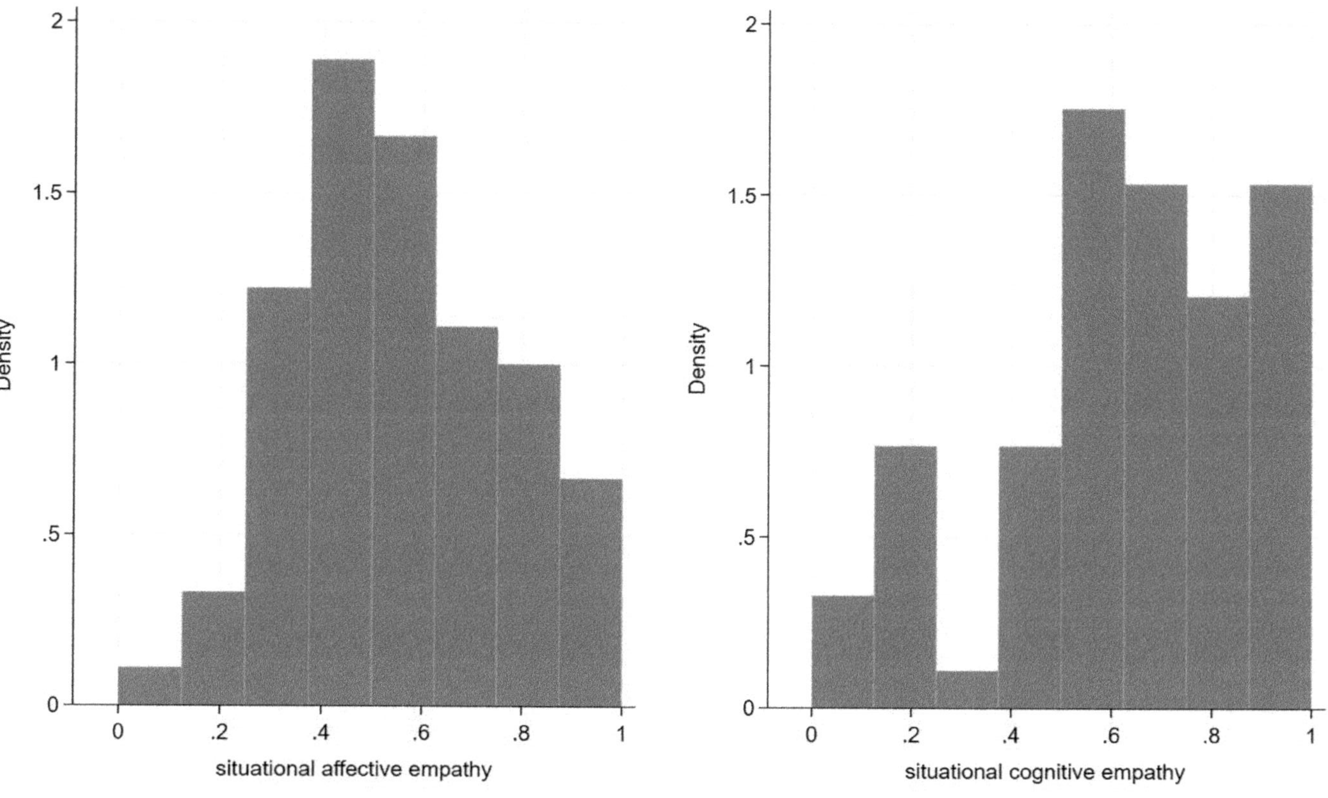

Figure 7 Situational empathy experienced by deliberators

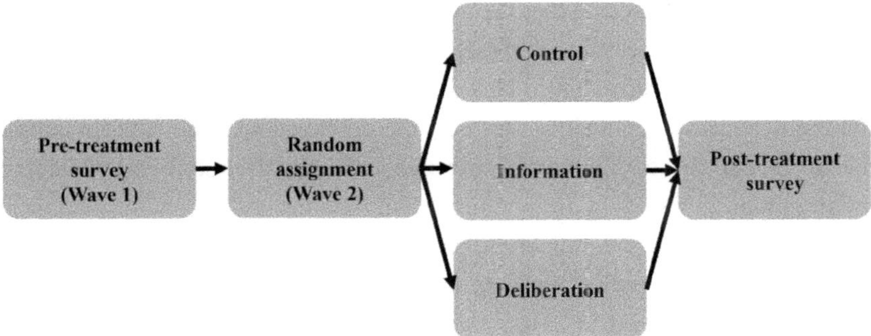

Figure 8 Study 4 design

found in media discussions. Following the reading, they were instructed to answer questions measuring the variables of interest. The purpose of designing this condition was to disentangle the effects of mere informational exposure from those of small-group deliberation.

Subjects who were randomly assigned to the deliberation group were invited to take part in a small-group discussion. To ensure that information provision remained constant, participants were first instructed to read a brief text about legalizing assisted dying in the UK, identical to the one given to the subjects in the information group. They were then directed to the seminar room, where they participated in a group discussion facilitated by a moderator. Each discussion group comprised eight to twelve participants, and the discussions lasted between 45 and 70 minutes. The design of the small-group deliberations included several key conditions: the provision of balanced information, the presence of a facilitator, establishing deliberative rules for discussions, encouragement to utilize various communicative tools, and exposure to diverse perspectives. Finally, those randomly assigned to the control condition received a short survey to complete.

Sample: For the Wave 1 survey, the subjects ($N = 600$) were 55 percent students and 45 percent nonstudents, recruited using a social sciences laboratory of a UK university. Among these participants, 68 percent were female, with 55 percent falling within the age group of 18 to 26, and 32 percent holding at least an undergraduate degree or equivalent (with approximately 0.5 percent having no formal qualifications). This sample was notably more diverse than the Belgian sample.

A total of 127 subjects participated at Wave 2: $N = 37$ in the deliberation, $N = 59$ in the placebo and $N = 31$ in the control conditions. Sixty participants were invited to take part in the experiment for both the information and deliberation groups. However, there were dropouts, particularly in the deliberation condition.

Post-hoc analyses indicated that the attrition was not systematic with respect to socio-demographic variables or baseline attitudes toward assisted dying. The dropouts were primarily due to heavy snowfall on the day of the discussions and the potentially demanding nature of the deliberations. The smaller sample size for the control condition was intentional, reflecting the relatively low interest in that group.

Measure: To capture reflection, in this study, I use Weinmann's (2018) psychometric self-reported measure for the concept of "deliberation within." The battery is designed to assess the cognitive information processing steps involved in reflective political reasoning, as predicted by the normative ideals of deliberative democracy. Respondents are asked to self-report on a 7-point scale, where "1" means "strongly disagree" and "7" means "strongly agree," how each of five items, (a) reassessing the biases favoring or opposing different arguments, (b) taking responsibility for making up one's own mind about the topic, after having heard the arguments of others; (c) simulating several opinions about the topic, (d) thinking about the arguments for and against ones' own as well as others' opinion, and (e) evaluating the arguments that speak for and against own as well as others' opinions, describe the development of thought processes during and after either having deliberated in a group (deliberation condition), read the text (information condition), or forming their opinion (control condition). The results of the factor analyses indicated that the first two items did not load effectively onto a single deliberation within variable. Consequently, a summary index was created from the remaining three items (alpha = 0.75; M = 16; SD = 3; range: 6–21) and was subsequently standardized using the control group's mean and standard deviation.[21]

Results: Table 4 reports the means and standard deviations of reflective political thinking across three experimental conditions.

Table 4 Reflective political reasoning

	Mean	SD	N
Control	0.00	1.00	31
Information	0.50	0.69	58
Deliberation	0.59	0.95	37

---

[21] This experiment was also reported in Muradova (2020). Yet the analytical strategy in Muradova (2020) differed from the current strategy along two dimensions. First, in Muradova (2020), despite a low Cronbach's alpha, an index of all five items was created. Second, in the original study, the outcome variable was standardized by sample mean and standard deviation. For experimental studies, the common practice is to standardize it by control mean and SD, which I adopt here.

The results of the difference-in-means *t*-tests indicate that both small-group deliberation and information provision have a statistically significant effect on individuals' tendency to engage in reflective political reasoning compared to the control condition. The effect size for information provision is equivalent to half a SD, while small-group deliberation yields an effect size of slightly more than half a SD, at two-tailed significance levels of $p < 0.01$ and $p < 0.02$ respectively. Having been exposed to cross-cutting arguments and views on legalizing assisted dying either by reading information or deliberating about it in small groups increases the reflectiveness of people's political reasoning on the issue. As the table shows, the mean reflection is larger in the deliberation group (0.09 SD greater, compared to the information condition). Yet, this effect is not statistically significant at conventional significance levels, potentially due to the sample size.

6.4 Study 5: A Survey Experiment in Chile and the UK

Design: Study 5 investigates the scalability of the reflection-inducing effects of deliberation on a larger public. At the core of deliberative institutions is exposure to cross-cutting views (Mutz 2002). This study is designed to isolate this component of deliberation and assess whether exposure to cross-cutting perspectives, in the absence of the affective and discursive elements of small-group deliberation, can similarly promote reflection and influence individuals' political attitude formation.

I conducted an online survey experiment where participants were exposed to either a conflicting perspective (disagreement condition) or an aligned perspective (agreement condition) on the issue of universal basic income. The treatment consisted of a vignette featuring a hypothetical couple, outlining their views on UBI and presenting arguments either for or against the introduction of the UBI scheme in the UK or Chile.

Sample: The experiment was a part of a larger study by Nuffield College Comparative Time-Sharing Experiments (CTSE) and was fielded in the spring of 2019 (UK) and winter of 2020 (Chile) in two online subject pools of the Centre for Experimental Social Sciences (CESS) of the University of Oxford. Both the UK sample ($N = 215$) and the Chile sample ($N = 208$) are descriptively diverse, but non-probability samples.

Measure: Similar to Study 3 (Belgium), I operationalize reflection with the *cognitive complexity* of political thinking, which concerns the degree to which a text conveys multidimensional as opposed to unidimensional reasoning. Individuals were first asked about their views on four different policy issues, in the form of a battery: legalizing assisted dying, investment in mental health services, introducing a universal basic income scheme, and obligatory military service (the latter was replaced by the issue of "reforming the pension system" for Chilean sample). The order of policy issues was randomized. Individual attitudes on universal basic income scheme (M_{uk} = 4.33; SD_{uk} = 1.66; M_{chile} = 4.05; SD_{chile} = 1.8; response scale: 1"strongly" – 6"strongly favor") were measured with a one-item tapping in respondents' approval of the scheme and proceeded by a short description of the scheme (adapted from ESS 2016). This was measured twice: pre- and post-treatment. Individuals were further asked to provide justification for their choice on introducing a *basic income* scheme. The exact question was as follows: "You indicated that you \${D_1/ChoiceGroup/SelectedAnswers/3}[22] introducing a basic income scheme in the UK/Chile. Why do you think so? Please justify your choice in one paragraph." Their essays were further coded for cognitive complexity score (standardized $M = 0$; SD = 1; range –1.8 to 2.5).

Results: The results of a manipulation test show that political disagreement was manipulated successfully in both UK and Chilean samples ($M_{agreeUK}$ = 0.02, $M_{disagreeUK}$ = 0.95; $p < 0.00$; $M_{agreeChile}$ = 0.11; $M_{disagreeChile}$ = 0.87; $p < 0.00$). I estimate the effect of exposure to cross-cutting views on reflective political reasoning with simple difference-in-means t-tests. Table 5 lists the mean and standard deviations of reflective thinking in each condition by country.

As the findings show, I cannot reject the null hypothesis that the effect of political disagreement on cognitive complexity is different from zero. Exposure to cross-cutting views per se exerts a null effect on the reflectiveness of people's political judgments, in both Chilean and UK samples. Although

Table 5 Reflective political reasoning

	Mean	**SD**	*N*
	UK		
Placebo	0.00	1.00	106
Treatment (cross-cutting)	−0.09	1.22	109
	Chile		
Placebo	0.00	1.00	104
Treatment (cross-cutting)	0.05	1.12	104

---

[22] Their chosen response was generated by a piped text function of the Qualtrics.

exposure to cross-cutting views appears to decrease cognitive complexity scores on average in the UK and increase them in Chile, neither effect is statistically significant. This provides an additional suggestive empirical support for the idea that the reflection-inducing potential of interpersonal deliberation may depend on its other, more affective dimensions.

6.5 Discussion

Study 3 (Belgium) shows that discussing legalizing assisted dying in small groups has a within-subject positive effect on the reflectiveness of individuals' political thinking. In a similar vein, Study 4 (UK) demonstrates that small-group deliberation can enhance reflective political thinking. However, exposure to information about the issue, along with a balanced presentation of arguments, can also have similarly positive effects. Although the effect of deliberation is greater than that of the information effect, the difference between these two effects is not statistically significant. This may be due to the smaller size of the sample. In Study 5 (UK and Chile), I isolate one element of small-group deliberation – exposure to cross-cutting view – and study its direct effect on the reflectiveness of people's political judgments and find that it exerts a null effect. To sum up, the first two studies show the potential of deliberation and balanced information provision to enhance the reflectiveness of people's political judgments. The last study demonstrates that mere exposure to an opposing perspective on the issue of universal basic income fails to influence political thinking.

It is challenging to approximate the small-group deliberation designed at lab settings or online to that of the real-world deliberative institutions. While the presence of diverse perspectives is crucial for fostering high-quality interpersonal deliberation, individuals in laboratory settings often lack sufficient time to form meaningful connections, engage in empathetic reflections, and build rapport. This absence of a nurturing environment may inhibit their ability to transcend biased political thinking, making it difficult for them to incorporate and integrate opposing viewpoints into their reasoning. Without the opportunity for these essential social interactions, the potential for deeper understanding and more comprehensive deliberation may be significantly diminished. Experiments with interpersonal deliberation of longer duration have been demonstrated to yield more robust positive democratic outcomes (e.g., Fishkin et al. 2021; Grönlund et al. 2015). Future research should take this into account in designing laboratory experiments approximating participation in a deliberative institution.

7 Discussion and Conclusion

7.1 Contributions

This Element makes three main contributions to the relevant literatures. First, it contributes to the long-standing academic debate about the nature of desirable political attitudes. I show that one way of evaluating the quality of citizens' political reasoning is to capture its reflectiveness – the extent to which people actively consider and integrate diverse and opposing perspectives in their thinking processes when forming their political beliefs. Understanding reflection and the institutional and noninstitutional ways via which it can be encouraged and nurtured has implications for the quality and resilience of democracies. Reflection has been shown to promote democratic accountability, by alleviating affective polarization, and partisan-motivated political attitudes (Arceneaux and Vander Wielen 2017; Brader and Tucker 2018) and leading to higher-quality political decisions (Fournier et al. 2011; Luskin et al. 2002). Engaging in reflection on political issues – regardless of persuasion – can motivate individuals to grasp the underlying rationales of policy decisions and to appreciate the perspectives of those who support them, even when those views oppose their own. As such, reflection can alleviate political conflict when individuals would gain less out of a policy decision. Furthermore, the habit of reflecting before forming political attitudes can make citizens more open and tolerant to opposing perspectives in the future, with beneficial implications for outgroup hostility and biases. Rather than outright dismissing the arguments presented by our political opponents, we can cultivate a greater inclination to pause and reflect on their viewpoints before assessing their persuasiveness. In a context where populist and right-wing politicians are making increasingly compelling appeals worldwide, it becomes normatively essential for citizens to be motivated to reflect on diverse and opposing perspectives instead of merely succumbing to them.

My contribution about reflection is also methodological. A significant portion of the political science literature on public opinion has concentrated on attitude transformation, the acquisition of factual knowledge, and information-seeking behaviors as key indicators of "good political decisions." (see also Druckman 2014). While it is much easier to measure them empirically, they fall short of capturing the cognitive steps individuals take to contemplate and integrate diverse and opposing perspectives in their thinking processes. Although not a perfect proxy for reflective thinking, cognitive complexity of thinking can be an interesting way of indirectly capturing the quality of people's judgments (see also Colombo 2018).

Second, I show that situational empathy for the other side can engender more reflective thinking. While the potential of empathy for other political outcomes, such as intergroup prejudice, altruism, affective polarization, intergroup support, and political ambition, has been studied, this Element theorizes and tests the role of situational empathy in encouraging individuals to go beyond their biased political reasoning and engage in reflection. My findings show that empathy for the other side is a powerful emotion that can promote political reflection. These findings have important implications for the literature on AIT (Marcus 2010; Marcus et al. 2000). This Element challenges the previously held belief that only negative emotions engender reflective political judgments. I demonstrate that, in the context of political disagreement, empathy can help individuals move beyond simply dismissing opposing views and engage in thoughtful reflection. Elsewhere, in the context of correcting misperceptions about climate change, I find the magnitude of the positive effect of empathy on people's accurate political judgments to be comparable to that of anxiety (Muradova, Michalaki, and Tsakiris 2024). Both emotions enhance people's willingness to correct their misperceptions. This highlights the critical role of empathy as an important emotion in understanding reflective political thinking.

This Element departs from previous studies that focus on the dark side of empathy (Bloom 2017; Simas et al. 2020). In contrast to these studies, this Element focuses on situational empathy instead of dispositional empathy. I build on the premise that social contexts can either activate or depress people's empathic reactions, with certain environments exerting a strong influence on individuals' inclination to empathize with others (Cheng et al. 2017). Research shows that the activation of individuals' empathy depends on various factors, including the nature of interpersonal relationships and the motivations of the empathizer (Stüber 2019). Moreover, in the existing political science literature, dispositional empathy is typically measured through self-reported responses to a series of items. However, prior research indicates that individuals often lack accurate meta-knowledge about their own empathic abilities, making dispositional measures likely to be poor predictors of actual empathic accuracy (Ickes 1993, 603; Ickes 2003). Third, studies asserting that empathy negatively impacts important democratic outcomes, such as political polarization, primarily concentrate on one dimension of empathy (i.e., empathic concern). In fact, Simas et al. (2020) finds that the cognitive dimension of dispositional empathy (i.e., perspective-taking) does *not* contribute to increased political polarization. I demonstrate that empathy for the other side, encompassing both affective and cognitive dimensions, fosters greater (not lesser) reflective political thinking in individuals.

Third, I argue that when designed properly, deliberative institutions, such as citizens' assemblies, can cultivate an environment conducive to eliciting empathy for the other side. I marshal a set of original qualitative, and experimental data to test the plausibility of this theoretical idea. First, I rely on a real-world and influential institution, the Irish Citizens' Assembly (2016–2018). My qualitative data shows that citizens' assemblies have the potential to nurture political environments where people spend time with different others, leading to the development of affective bonds and mutual trust among participants. In these processes, the presence of diversity of viewpoints and arguments is important.

Affective engagement encourages individuals to be more receptive to new information and diverse, opposing perspectives, whether conveyed through factual arguments or personal stories and testimonies, ultimately enhancing their empathy toward others. It is the empathy for other side that motivates individuals to engage in more demanding processes of reflection. My focus on deliberative institutions here is distinct from prior work investigating reflection-enhancing potential of interpersonal deliberation. An overwhelming majority of prior studies have mostly focused on the cognitive causal mechanisms – such as knowledge acquisition and persuasion through the Habermasian force of the better argument – underpinning small-group discussion and their potentially beneficial outcomes.[23] Deliberative democrats have usually emphasized the reason-giving and learning aspects of interpersonal deliberation in these processes. This Element focuses on an affective mechanism. Learning, and deliberating are intertwined with deliberative institution's capacity to create emotional bonding and empathetic engagement both during and beyond small-group discussions. My hope is that the theoretical argument presented in this Element can serve as an inspiration for deliberation scholars to develop their own testable and generalizable theories about the role of affect in deliberation.

Furthermore, I substantiate my argument about the relationship between interpersonal deliberation and reflective political reasoning with laboratory, and quasi-experiments. The findings relate to several different strands of research investigating the effects of political disagreement and small-group deliberation on individuals' political opinion formation and intergroup relations. First, the results with regards to the reflection-enhancing potential of interpersonal deliberation are consistent with recent experiments on deliberation. For example, Fishkin and colleagues (2021) employ a field experiment – America in One Room – to investigate the effect of participating in a deliberative forum on political polarization among Republicans and Democrats. Their findings reveal that interpersonal deliberation not only transforms individuals' policy attitudes but also reduces affective polarization.

---

[23] But see Lindell et al. (2017) and Saam (2018) for different perspectives.

Second, in the context of the Irish Citizens' Assembly, I find that one of the necessary design features of a deliberative institution for its empathy-inducing potential is the presence of diversity of perspectives. This finding relates to the argument in political science and communication that cross-cutting political conversations can enhance the quality of people's political judgments (Huckfeldt et al. 2004; Mutz 2002; but see Wojcieszak and Price 2010). In the context of discussions about energy and health care policies in the US, Samara Klar (2014) finds that heterogenous small-group discussions can exert a positive effect on individuals' political opinion formation by alleviating partisan-motivated reasoning, while homogenous group discussions tend to have a polarizing effect.

The findings of this Element give suggestive evidence that an affective causal mechanism (feeling empathy for the other side) may be responsible for positive relationship between cross-cutting political conversations and reflection. This Element also broadens the empirical scope of this strand of literature by moving beyond the predominantly studied country contexts, such as the US, to include data from four different countries – Belgium, Chile, Ireland, and the UK.

The findings of this Element can also help practitioners of deliberative minipublics design forums that enhance participants' reflective potential. Ensuring that empathy-sparking institutional features of deliberative minipublics (e.g., affective engagement, presence of diversity of perspectives, instructions that encourage active imagination) are present when organizing such institution can enhance the process of reflective political attitude formation among participants in democratic innovation institutions.

7.2 Limitations and Future Research

I readily admit that more research needs to be done to make a stronger case for the relationship between situational empathy and reflection, as well as deliberative institutions, empathy, and reflective political thinking. For instance, critics may wonder whether empathy would function differently in highly partisan contexts. As I showed (with qualitative data) in the case of the ICA deliberations on highly divisive and partisan issue of abortion, empathy has potential to bridge the partisan divide and encourage more considered political judgments. However, none of my experimental studies incorporate or manipulate partisan context in their design. In Study 1, I don't prime the partisanship of the target of empathy. In the experiments involving small-group deliberation (Studies 3 and 4), individuals' party affiliations are not made salient. Future research should examine the relationship between empathy, partisanship, and reflection with different study designs. Alternatively, could deemphasizing partisanship in political interactions be a way to encourage empathy and reflective political thinking in individuals?

This Element is not arguing that empathy is a panacea for politics. Empathy can be biased, costly, and cognitively demanding, particularly when directed toward strangers (Cameron et al. 2019). Under certain conditions, it may lead to in-group favoritism, and enhanced stereotyping, and it can also be a risk factor for psychopathic and manipulative tendencies among citizens (Ferguson 2016). Although most of these theorized negative outcomes of empathy pertain to trait-level dispositional empathy (rather than situational empathy), I believe future research should explore which social contexts exacerbate and which alleviate the potential dark side of empathy in political disagreement and conflict.

Other interesting questions remain to be answered. What happens when we are motivated to empathize with someone who holds undemocratic political beliefs and policy preferences? Or what if the opposing perspective someone is trying to consider is factually inaccurate? For example, what if we are motivated to empathize with a person holding strong misperceptions about the anthropogenic cause of the climate change? According to my theory's predictions, this may lead individuals to contemplate opposing perspectives, but it won't necessarily result in a transformation of their existing beliefs. Future research could experimentally manipulate the source and nature of opposing perspectives to explore these and other relevant questions.

Moreover, how durable are the reflection-inducing effects of empathy and deliberative forums? Are these effects short-lived or do they persist? The studies presented in this Element do not study the long-term effects of empathy and deliberative forums on people's political judgments. Another important avenue is to examine whether individual characteristics, such as dispositional empathy, moderate the effect of empathy and deliberative institutions on people's political opinion formation (see, for instance, Clifford et al. 2019).

7.3 Scaling Up Interpersonal Deliberation?

If deliberative processes can effectively bridge political divides and make people more empathetic and reflective in their political opinion formation, how can we extend such effects to a larger group of citizens? Some scholars have been advocating for institutionalizing deliberative processes (Setälä 2017). There are different ideas among the scholars and practitioners alike. Some advocate for radical changes, such as replacing conventional political institutions with citizens-centered deliberative forums (Landemore 2020), while others propose introducing new legislatures, like replacing the second chamber of parliaments with citizen-centered institutions (Gastil and Wright 2019; van Reybrouck 2016).

A guide by the Organization for Economic Cooperation and Development proposes eight different ways of including representative public deliberation in political decision-making processes (Chwalisz 2021). One of these ideas has already been implemented in practice: the Permanenter Bürgerdialog (PBD) (2019), a permanent citizens' assembly established in Ostbelgien, the German-speaking federal entity of Belgium. The PBD consists of randomly selected citizens who discuss the issues on the agenda of the parliament and work in collaboration with the parliament to implement them into public policy (Macq and Jacquet 2023).

While deliberative institutions can undoubtedly contribute to democratic processes, they are by no means a cure-all for the myriad challenges facing contemporary democracies. When organized inadequately, such institutions may have pernicious effects. One pattern that emerged from my ICA qualitative data suggests that when there is a lack of a clear link with the political decision-making, engagement in these processes may lead to frustration among participants, and the institution's credibility may be jeopardized (e.g., Germann et al. 2024; see also Muradova and Suiter 2022). The French Citizens' Convention for Climate,[24] an influential citizens' assembly provides an interesting illustrative case for it. Only 10 percent of its recommendations were taken up by the French government with no modification, with the rest either being rejected (53 percent) or modified (37 percent) (Courant 2021). The French president's backtracking on honoring the convention's recommendations led to disappointments and a loss of political trust among participants (Courant 2021; Trian 2021). Hence, before embarking on ambitious endeavors with regards to organizing deliberative minipublics, we must first garner a more comprehensive understanding of the effects of these institutions through additional and more systematic research.

Furthermore, it is also practically challenging to involve all citizenry in small-group deliberations in large-scale societies. Some of my findings (i.e., Study 4) show that under some conditions, provision of balanced information (both pro and con arguments on the issue of legalizing assisted dying) can similarly contribute to reflectiveness of people's political judgments. Elsewhere, we find that when members of the wider public – those not participating in interpersonal deliberation – are exposed to statements for and against a policy issue emanating from a deliberative minipublic, such as during the referendum on blasphemy in

---

[24] The Convention was established following the "yellow vest movement" sweeping France in 2018 and lasted between October 2019 to June 2020.

Ireland, they report feeling more empathy for the opposing side (Suiter et al. 2020). To the extent that this way of providing information about the issue can work well across different country and issue contexts, it could be a cost-effective strategy for eliciting empathy for the other side in individuals.

7.4 Concluding Remarks

> If we hope to meet the moral test of our times, we're going to have to talk more about the empathy deficit, the ability to see ourselves when we choose to empathize with the plight of others. It is time for a sense of empathy to infuse our politics in America.
>
> *Barack Obama, December 04, 2006*

> […] be really driven by empathy. […] When you think about all the big challenges that we face in the world. … We need our leaders to be able to empathize with the circumstances of others … to empathize with the next generation that we're making decisions on behalf of.
>
> *Jacinda Ardern, for Guardian, May 30, 2020*

This Element is an attempt to advance our understanding of the emotional and institutional ways of motivating more reflective political reasoning. Arguably, its main lesson is that citizens are not inherently biased; given the right opportunity and motivation, they are willing to transcend their biases and make more considerate political choices. The current democratic institutions may create little motivation for citizens to engage in reflective political reasoning. The lack of adequate structures and motivations, however, is not indicative of inherent deficiency in individuals' ability to reflect (Groenendyk and Krupnikov 2021).

Empathy has been championed by scholars across different disciplines and by prominent political figures, as illustrated by quotes from former U.S. President Barack Obama and former New Zealand Prime Minister Jacinda Ardern at the beginning of this section. Research shows that empathy is a motivated response; under the right conditions, most people are capable of empathizing with diverse others (Zaki 2018). This Element argues that empathy for the other side can foster normatively desirable democratic outcomes, such as reflective political thinking. In an increasingly polarized world, empathy for the other can promote respectful and other-regarding political interactions and political reasoning. If different environments and institutions can be designed in a way that potential bias in empathy can be minimized or overcome, motivating us to actively exercise our empathetic capacities, why not aspire to attain this goal in our societies? As spaces for political bonding, and conversation, minipublics can provide institutional processes for eliciting political empathy for the other side, with implications for the quality of political judgments. Yet, how would we transfer the empathy-inducing benefits of interpersonal deliberation into institutions which are not predefined as deliberative? I believe the scholars of institutional design should explore the ways via which empathy can be institutionalized within existing conventional political institutions. Crawford (2014) argues for the institutionalization of empathy in world politics via empathetic diplomacy, and cultural interactions. Jennings and colleagues (2019, 509) see museums as organizations that should possess institutional empathy, which they define as "building awareness of and holding space for the deep-seated needs and experiences of their surrounding communities."

Cultivating a sense of community, a habit of political conversation among citizens, and creating opportunities for everyday talk between diverse others could be a way of nurturing empathy for the other side and promoting reflective thinking among individuals. Civil society can play an important role in such initiatives.

The increasing appeal of extreme right-wing parties and candidates, coupled with nascent populism, and the pervasive spread of mis- and disinformation around the world accentuate the imperative to study whether societies and institutions can be organized to provide citizens with opportunities and motivation to make more reflective political decisions. This Element represents one such attempt.

References

Achen, C., & Bartels, L. (2016). *Democracy for realists: Why elections do not produce responsive government.* Princeton, NJ: Princeton University Press.

Allport, G. W. (1954). *The nature of prejudice.* Reading, MA: Addison-Wesley.

Arceneaux, K., & Vander Wielen, R. J. (2017). *Taming intuition: How reflection minimizes partisan reasoning and promotes democratic accountability.* Cambridge: Cambridge University Press.

Arendt, H. (1989). *Lectures on Kant's political philosophy.* Chicago, IL: University of Chicago Press.

Bakker, B. N., Lelkes, Y., & Malka, A. (2020). Understanding partisan cue receptivity: Tests of predictions from the bounded rationality and expressive utility perspectives. *The Journal of Politics, 82*(3), 1061–1077.

Bartels, L. M. (2002). Beyond the running tally: Partisan bias in political perceptions. *Political Behavior, 24,* 117–150.

Batson, C. D. (2010). *Altruism in humans.* Oxford: Oxford University Press.

Beiner, R. (1983). *Political judgment.* London: Methuen.

Bidadanure, J. U. (2019). The political theory of universal basic income. *Annual Review of Political Science, 22,* 481–501.

Black, L. W. (2008). Deliberation, storytelling, and dialogic moments. *Communication Theory, 18,* 93–116.

Bloom, P. (2017). *Against empathy: The case for rational compassion.* New York City, NY: Random House.

Bottoni, G. (2023). *CROss-National Online Survey 2 (CRONOS-2) panel data and documentation user guide.* London: ESS ERIC.

Brader, T., & Marcus, G. E. (2013). Emotion and political psychology. In L. Huddy, D. O. Sears, & J. S. Levy (eds.), *The Oxford handbook of political psychology,* Second Ed. Oxford: Oxford University Press (165–204).

Brader, T., & Tucker, J. A. (2018). Unreflective partisans? Policy information and evaluation in the development of partisanship. *Political Psychology, 39,* 137–157.

Brader, T., Valentino, N. A., & Suhay, E. (2008). What triggers public opposition to immigration? Anxiety, group cues, and immigration threat. *American Journal of Political Science, 52*(4), 959–978.

Broockman, D., & Kalla, J. (2016). Durably reducing transphobia: A field experiment on door-to-door canvassing. *Science, 352*(6282), 220–224.

Brophy, N., & Mullinix, K. J. (2024). Partisan motivated empathy and policy attitudes. *Political Behavior, 46*(3), 1701–1723.

Brundidge, J., Reid, S. A., Choi, S., & Muddiman, A. (2014). The "deliberative digital divide": Opinion leadership and integrative complexity in the US political blogosphere. *Political Psychology, 35*(6), 741–755.

Bullock, J. G., Gerber, A. S., Hill, S. J., & Huber, G. A. (2015). Partisan bias in factual beliefs about politics. *Quarterly Journal of Political Science, 10*(4), 519–578.

Cameron, C. D., Hutcherson, C. A., Ferguson, A. M., et al. (2019). Empathy is hard work: People choose to avoid empathy because of its cognitive costs. *Journal of Experimental Psychology, 148*(6), 962.

Campbell, A., Converse, P. E., Miller, W. E., & Stokes, D. E. (1960). *The American voter.* New York: Wiley.

Carswell, S. (2017). Citizens' assembly: Reaction from both sides of abortion debate, 23 April, www.irishtimes.com/news/ireland/irish-news/citizens-assembly-reaction-from-both-sides-of-abortion-debate-1.3058645.

Cheng, Y., Chen, C., & Decety, J. (2017). How situational context impacts empathic responses and brain activation patterns. *Frontiers in Behavioral Neuroscience, 11*, 165.

Chwalisz, C. (2021). Eight ways to institutionalise deliberative democracy, OECD Public Governance Policy Papers, No.12, December 14, www.oecd.org/gov/open-government/eight-ways-to-institutionalise-deliberative-democracy.htm.

Cikara, M., Bruneau, E. G., & Saxe, R. R. (2011). Us and them: Intergroup failures of empathy. *Current Directions in Psychological Science, 20*(3), 149–153.

Clifford, S., Kirkland, J. H., & Simas, E. N. (2019). How dispositional empathy influences political ambition. *The Journal of Politics, 81*(3), 1043–1056.

Colombo, C. (2018). Hearing the other side? Debiasing political opinions in the case of the Scottish independence referendum. *Political Studies, 66*(1), 23–42.

Connors, E. C., Pietryka, M. T., & Ryan, J. B. (2022). *Examining motivations in interpersonal communication experiments.* Cambridge: Cambridge University Press.

Converse, P. E. (1964). The nature of belief systems in mass publics. In D. E. Apter (ed.), *Ideology and discontent.* New York: Free Press (206–261).

Courant, D. (2021). The promises and disappointments of the French citizens' convention for climate. Deliberative Democracy Digest, June 9. www.publicdeliberation.net/the-promises-and-disappointments-of-the-french-citizens-convention-for-climate/.

Crawford, N. C. (2014). Institutionalizing passion in world politics: Fear and empathy. *International Theory, 6*(3), 535–557.

Curato, N. (2019). *Democracy in a time of misery: From spectacular tragedies to deliberative action*. Oxford: Oxford University Press.

Curato, N., & Farrell, D. (2021). *Deliberative mini-publics: Core design features*. Bristol: Policy Press.

Dahl, R. (1971). *Polyarchy: Participation and opposition*. New Haven, CT: Yale University Press.

Davis, M. H. (1983). Measuring individual differences in empathy: Evidence for a multidimensional approach. *Journal of Personality and Social Psychology, 44*, 113–126.

Decety, J. (2012). *Empathy: From bench to bedside*. Cambridge, MA: MIT Press.

De Waal, F. B. (2012). Empathy in primates and other mammals. In J. Decety (ed.), *Empathy: From bench to bedside*. Cambridge, MA: MIT Press (87–106).

Dewey, J. (1933). *How we think: A restatement of the relation of reflective thinking to the educative process*. Boston, MA: D.C. Heath.

Druckman, J. N. (2012). The politics of motivation. *Critical Review, 24*(2), 199–216.

Druckman, J. N. (2014). Pathologies of studying public opinion, political communication, and democratic responsiveness. *Political Communication, 31*(3), 467–492.

Elstub, S. (2014). Deliberative pragmatic equilibrium review: A framework for comparing institutional devices and their enactment of deliberative democracy in the UK. *The British Journal of Politics and International Relations, 16*(3), 386–409.

Epley, N., & Caruso, E. M. (2009). Perspective taking: Misstepping into others shoes. In K. D. Markman, W. M. P. Klein, J. A. Suhr (eds.), *Handbook of imagination and mental simulation*. Hove: Psychology Press (297–311).

Erle, T. M., & Topolinski, S. (2017). The grounded nature of psychological perspective-taking. *Journal of Personality and Social Psychology, 112*(5), 683.

ESS (European Social Survey). (2016). ESS Round 8: European Social Survey Round 8 Data. Norwegian Centre for Research Data, Norway.

Esterling, K. M., Neblo, M. A., & Lazer, D. M. (2011). Means, motive, and opportunity in becoming informed about politics: A deliberative field experiment with members of Congress and their constituents. *Public Opinion Quarterly, 75*(3), 483–503.

Farrell, D. M., Suiter, J., Cunningham, K., & Harris, C. (2023). When mini-publics and maxi-publics coincide: Ireland's national debate on abortion. *Representation, 59*(1), 55–73.

Ferguson, E. (2016). Empathy: "The good, the bad and the ugly". In A. M. Wood & J. Johnson (eds.), *The Wiley handbook of positive clinical psychology*. Wiley-Blackwell (103–123).

Fishkin, J., Siu, A., Diamond, L., & Bradburn, N. (2021). Is deliberation an antidote to extreme partisan polarization? Reflections on "America in one room." *American Political Science Review, 115*(4), 1464–1481.

Fishkin, J. S. (1991). *Democracy and deliberation: New directions for democratic reform*. New Haven, Conn.: Yale University Press.

Fournier, P., Turgeon, M., Blais, A., et al. (2011). Deliberation from within: Changing one's mind during an interview. *Political Psychology, 32*(5), 885–919.

Fung, A. (2003). Recipes for public spheres: Eight institutional design choices and their consequences. *Journal of Political Philosophy, 11, 338*, 345.

Gadarian, S. K., & Albertson, B. (2014). Anxiety, immigration, and the search for information. *Political Psychology, 35*(2), 133–164.

Galinsky, A. D., & Moskowitz, G. B. (2000). Perspective-taking: Decreasing stereotype expression, stereotype accessibility, and in-group favoritism. *Journal of Personality and Social Psychology, 78*(4), 708.

Gastil, J. (2008). *Political communication and deliberation*. Los Angeles, CA: Sage.

Gastil, J. (2018). The lessons and limitations of experiments in democratic deliberation. *Annual Review of Law and Social Science, 14*, 271–291.

Gastil, J., & Wright, E. O. (eds.) (2019). *Legislature by lot: Transformative designs for deliberative governance*. London: Verso Books.

Germann, M., Marien, S., & Muradova, L. (2024). Scaling up? Unpacking the effect of deliberative mini-publics on legitimacy perceptions. *Political Studies, 72*(2), 677–700.

Gerring, J. (2004). What is a case study and what is it good for? *American Political Science Review, 98*(2), 341–354.

Goodin, R. E. (2003). *Reflective democracy*. Oxford: Oxford University Press.

Groenendyk, E., & Krupnikov, Y. (2021). What motivates reasoning? A theory of goal-dependent political evaluation. *American Journal of Political Science, 65*(1), 180–196.

Grönlund, K., Herne, K., & Setälä, M. (2015). Does enclave deliberation polarize opinions? *Political Behavior, 37*, 995–1020.

Grönlund, K., Herne, K., & Setälä, M. (2017). Empathy in a citizen deliberation experiment. *Scandinavian Political Studies, 40*(4), 457–480.

Guess, A., & Coppock, A. (2020). Does counter-attitudinal information cause backlash? Results from three large survey experiments. *British Journal of Political Science, 50*(4), 1497–1515.

Habermas, J. (1996). *Between facts and norms*. Cambridge, MA: MIT Press.

Huckfeldt, R., Mendez, J. M., & Osborn, T. (2004). Disagreement, ambivalence, and engagement: The political consequences of heterogeneous networks. *Political Psychology, 25*(1), 65–95.

Huddy, L., Mason, L., & Aarøe, L. (2015). Expressive partisanship: Campaign involvement, political emotion, and partisan identity. *American Political Science Review, 109*(1), 1–17.

Ickes, W. (1993). Empathic accuracy. *Journal of Personality, 61*(4), 587–610.

Ickes, W. (2003). *Everyday mind reading: Understanding what other people think and feel*. Amherst, NY: Prometheus Books.

Jacquet, V. (2017). Explaining non-participation in deliberative mini-publics. *European Journal of Political Research, 56*(3), 640–659.

Jennings, G., Cullen, J., Bryant, J., et al. (2019). The empathetic museum: A new institutional identity. *Curator: The Museum Journal, 62*(4), 505–526.

Johnson, G. F., Morrell, M. E., & Black, L. W. (2019). Emotions and deliberation in the citizens' initiative review. *Social Science Quarterly, 100*(6), 2168–2187.

Kalla, J. L., & Broockman, D. E. (2023). Which narrative strategies durably reduce prejudice? Evidence from field and survey experiments supporting the efficacy of perspective-getting. *American Journal of Political Science, 67*(1), 185–204.

Kam, C. D. (2006). Political campaigns and open-minded thinking. *The Journal of Politics, 68*(4), 931–945.

Kawulich, B. B. (2005). Participant observation as a data collection method. *Forum Qualitative Sozialforschung/Forum: Qualitative Social Research, 6* (2), Article 43.

Klar, S. (2014). Partisanship in a social setting. *American Journal of Political Science, 58*(3), 687–704.

Krause, S. R. (2008). *Civil passions: Moral sentiment and democratic deliberation*. Princeton: Princeton University Press.

Kunda, Z. (1990). The case for motivated reasoning. *Psychological Bulletin, 108*(3), 480.

Lacelle-Webster, A. (2024). "What should we hope for? Democratic hope and the collective, uncertain, and future-oriented dimensions of democratic politics." A conference paper presented at Yale ISPS conference "Deliberative Democracy with a passion: Identities, emotions, and the formation of political judgement," May 16, 2024.

Landemore, H. (2020). *Open democracy: Reinventing popular rule for the twenty-first century*. Princeton: Princeton University Press.

Landemore, H. (2024). "Truth and love in politics." A conference paper presented at Yale ISPS conference "Deliberative Democracy with a passion: Identities, emotions, and the formation of political judgement," May 16, 2024.

Lindell, M., Bächtiger, A., Grönlund, K., et al. (2017). What drives the polarisation and moderation of opinions? Evidence from a Finnish citizen deliberation experiment on immigration. *European Journal of Political Research*, *56*(1), 23–45.

Luskin, R. C., Fishkin, J. S., & Jowell, R. (2002). Considered opinions: Deliberative polling in Britain. *British Journal of Political Science*, *32*(3), 455–487.

Macq, H., & Jacquet, V. (2023). Institutionalising participatory and deliberative procedures: The origins of the first permanent citizens' assembly. *European Journal of Political Research*, *62*(1), 156–173.

Mansbridge, J. J. (1983). *Beyond adversary democracy*. Chicago: University of Chicago Press.

Marcus, G. E. (2010). *Sentimental citizen: Emotion in democratic politics*. University Park, PA: Penn State Press.

Marcus, G. E., Neuman, W. R., & MacKuen, M. (2000). *Affective intelligence and political judgment*. Chicago: University of Chicago Press.

Marlborough, A. (2016). Irish constitutional debate on abortion and the resort to Citizens' Assemblies 23 August, https://constitutionnet.org/news/irish-con stitutional-debate-abortion-and-resort-citizens-assemblies.

McCullough, M. E., Worthington, E. L. Jr., & Rachal, K. C. (1997). Interpersonal forgiving in close relationships. *Journal of Personality and Social Psychology*, *73*(2), 321–336.

McDonald, J. (2023). *Feeling their pain: Why voters want leaders who care*. Oxford: Oxford University Press.

Mendelberg, T. (2002). The deliberative citizen: Theory and evidence. *Political Decision Making, Deliberation and Participation*, *6*(1), 151–193.

Mercier, H., & Landemore, H. (2012). Reasoning is for arguing: Understanding the successes and failures of deliberation. *Political Psychology*, *33*(2), 243–258.

Morrell, M. E. (2010). *Empathy and democracy: Feeling, thinking, and deliberation*. University Park, PA: Penn State Press.

Mullinix, K. J. (2018). Civic duty and political preference formation. *Political Research Quarterly*, *71*(1), 199–214.

Muradova, L. (2020). Seeing the other side? Perspective-taking and reflective political judgements in interpersonal deliberation. *Political Studies*, *69*(3), 644–664.

Muradova, L., & Arceneaux, K. (2022a). Political Belief Formation: Individual Differences and Situational Factors. In Musolino, J., Sommer, J., and Hemmer, P., the *Cognitive Science of Belief: A Multidisciplinary Approach*, Cambridge: Cambridge University Press (279–297).

Muradova, L., & Arceneaux, K. (2022b). Reflective political reasoning: Political disagreement and empathy. *European Journal of Political Research, 61*(3), 740–761.

Muradova, L., & Suiter, J. (2022). Public compliance with difficult political decisions in times of a pandemic: Does citizen deliberation help? *International Journal of Public Opinion Research, 34*(3), edac026.

Muradova, L., Walker, H., & Colli, F. (2020). Climate change communication and public engagement in interpersonal deliberative settings: Evidence from the Irish citizens' assembly. *Climate Policy, 20*(10), 1322–1335.

Muradova, L., Michalaki, K., & Tsakiris, M. (2024). Felling our way through misperceptions on climate change. Working paper.

Mutz, D. C. (2002). Cross-cutting social networks: Testing democratic theory in practice. *American Political Science Review, 96*(1), 111–126.

Neblo, M. A. (2020). Impassioned democracy: The roles of emotion in deliberative theory. *American Political Science Review, 114*(3), 923–927.

O'Shaughnessy, A. C. (2022). Triumph and concession? The moral and emotional construction of Ireland's campaign for abortion rights. *European Journal of Women's Studies, 29*(2), 233–249.

Owens, R. J., & Wedeking, J. P. (2011). Justices and legal clarity: Analyzing the complexity of U.S. supreme court opinions. *Law & Society Review, 45*(4), 1027–1061.

Penigaud, T. (2024). "Causes and reasons in voting behaviors." A conference paper presented at Yale ISPS conference "Deliberative democracy with a passion: Identities, emotions, and the formation of political judgement," May 16, 2024.

Pettigrew, T. F., & Tropp, L. R. (2006). A meta-analytic test of intergroup contact theory. *Journal of Personality and Social Psychology, 90*(5), 751.

Pettigrew, T. F., Tropp, L. R., Wagner, U., & Christ, O. (2011). Recent advances in intergroup contact theory. *International Journal of Intercultural Relations, 35*(3), 271–280.

Richards, R., Morrell, M. E., Brinker, D., Reedy, J., & Richards, Jr., R. C. (2022). Psychological phenomena in democratic deliberation. *Journal of Deliberative Democracy, 18*(2), 1–7.

Rosenberg, S. W. (2007). Rethinking democratic deliberation: The limits and potential of citizen participation. *Polity, 39*(3), 335–360.

Ryan, M. (2021). *Why citizen participation succeeds or fails: A comparative analysis of participatory budgeting.* Bristol: Policy Press.

Saam, N. J. (2018). Recognizing the emotion work in deliberation: Why emotions do not make deliberative democracy more democratic. *Political Psychology, 39*(4), 755–774.

Saunders, B., Sim, J., & Kingstone, T. (2018). Saturation in qualitative research: Exploring its conceptualization and operationalization. *Quality & Quantity, 52*(4), 1893–1907.

Setälä, M. (2017). Connecting deliberative mini-publics to representative decision making. *European Journal of Political Research, 56*(4), 846–863.

Simas, E. N., Clifford, S., & Kirkland, J. H. (2020). How empathic concern fuels political polarization. *American Political Science Review, 114*(1), 258–269.

Simonovits, G., Kezdi, G., & Kardos, P. (2018). Seeing the world through the other's eye: An online intervention reducing ethnic prejudice. *American Political Science Review, 112*(1), 186–193.

Sirin, C. V., Villalobos, J. D., & Valentino, N. A. (2016). Group empathy theory: The effect of group empathy on US intergroup attitudes and behavior in the context of immigration threats. *The Journal of Politics, 78*(3), 893–908.

Sirin, C. V., Valentino, N. A., & Villalobos, J. D. (2021). *Seeing us in them: Social divisions and the politics of group empathy.* Cambridge: Cambridge University Press.

Stüber, K. (2019). Measuring empathy. In E. N. Zalta (ed.), *The Stanford encyclopedia of philosophy* (https://plato.stanford.edu/entries/empathy/measuring.html). Stanford: The Metaphysics Research Lab, Stanford University.

Suedfeld, P. (2010). The cognitive processing of politics and politicians: Archival studies of conceptual and integrative complexity. *Journal of Personality, 78*(6), 1669–1702.

Suiter, J., Muradova, L., Gastil, J., & Farrell, D. M. (2020). Scaling up deliberation: Testing the potential of mini-publics to enhance the deliberative capacity of citizens. *Swiss Political Science Review, 26*(3), 253–272.

Taber, C. S., & Lodge, M. (2006). Motivated skepticism in the evaluation of political beliefs. *American Journal of Political Science, 50*(3), 755–769.

Tashakkori, A., & Teddlie, C. (2021). *Sage handbook of mixed methods in social & behavioral research.* Thousand Oaks, CA: Sage.

Tausczik, Y. R., & Pennebaker, J. W. (2010). The psychological meaning of words: LIWC and computerized text analysis methods. *Journal of Language and Social Psychology, 29*(1), 24–54.

Tetlock, P. E. (1983). Accountability and complexity of thought. *Journal of Personality and Social Psychology, 45*(1), 74–83.

Tetlock, P. E., Bernzweig, J., & Gallant, J. L. (1985). Supreme Court decision making: Cognitive style as a predictor of ideological consistency of voting. *Journal of Personality and Social Psychology, 48*(5), 1227.

Todd, A. R., & Galinsky, A. D. (2014). Perspective-taking as a strategy for improving intergroup relations: Evidence, mechanisms, and qualifications. *Social and Personality Psychology Compass, 8*(7), 374–387.

Todd, A. R., Bodenhausen, G. V., & Galinsky, A. D. (2012). Perspective taking combats the denial of intergroup discrimination. *Journal of Experimental Social Psychology, 48*(3), 738–745.

Trian, N. (2021). Macron's "direct democracy" to be tested as citizens' panel on climate wraps up, March 01, www.france24.com/en/france/20210301-macron-s-direct-democracy-to-be-tested-as-citizens-panel-on-climate-wraps-up.

Tuller, H. M., Bryan, C. J., Heyman, G. D., & Christenfeld, N. J. S. (2015). Seeing the other side: Perspective taking and the moderation of extremity. *Journal of Experimental Social Psychology, 59*, 18–23.

Turkenburg, E., & Goovaerts, I. (2024). Food for thought: A longitudinal investigation of reflection-promoting speech in televised election debates (1985–2019). *Political Studies, 72*(1), 67–89.

Ugarriza, J. E., & Nussio, E. (2017). The effect of perspective-giving on postconflict reconciliation. An experimental approach. *Political Psychology, 38*(1), 3–19.

Valli, C., & Nai, A. (2023). Dispositioned to resist? The Big Five and resistance to dissonant political views. *Personality and Individual Differences, 207*, 112152.

Van Reybrouck, D. (2016). *Against elections: The case for democracy.* London: The Bodley Head.

Webster, S. W., & Albertson, B. (2022). Emotion and politics: Noncognitive psychological biases in public opinion. *Annual Review of Political Science, 25*, 401–418.

Weinmann, C. (2018). Measuring political thinking: Development and validation of a scale for "deliberation within." *Political Psychology, 39*(2), 365–380.

Wojcieszak, M., & Price, V. (2010). Bridging the divide or intensifying the conflict? How disagreement affects strong predilections about sexual minorities. *Political Psychology, 31*(3), 315–339.

Wyss, D., Beste, S., & Bächtiger, A. (2015). A decline in the quality of debate? The evolution of cognitive complexity in Swiss parliamentary debates on immigration (1968–2014). *Swiss Political Science Review, 21*(4), 636–653.

Zaki, J. (2018). Empathy is a moral force. In K. Gray, & J. Graham (eds.), *Atlas of moral psychology.* New York City, NY: The Guilford Press (49–58).

Acknowledgments

This Element was only possible thanks to the support of many mentors, colleagues, and friends. Incredibly thankful to the former series editor Yanna Krupnikov for trusting me with this Element, and for her insightful feedback. The current series editor Liz Suhay and two anonymous reviewers were instrumental in helping me refine my ideas. This project benefited from invaluable feedback I received over the years from my mentors and friends Vin Arceneaux and Bert Bakker. I'm grateful to Michael Neblo for his kind email about my first publication as a PhD student and his advice on my book proposal, despite not knowing me personally. I'm immensely grateful to Nicole Curato, Sofie Marien, André Bächtiger, David Farrell, Michael Morrell, Robert Goodin, Andrea Felicetti, Diana Mutz, Shana Gadarian, Jane Suiter, Maija Setälä, Kaisa Herne, Manos Tsakiris, Jean Decety, Christopher Karpowitz, Matt Ryan, Edana Beauvais, Hélène Landemore, my PhD committee members, University of Leuven friends and colleagues and many other academics for their feedback on my ideas. The Element was revised during the first few months of my new faculty job at Southampton University and I'm grateful to my new wonderful colleagues for making me feel welcomed. Thanks also go to my girlfriends Laura, Hayley, Carmen, Tània, Amélie, Amy, Nieves, Ine, Catherine, and Lila for their love, support, and dance parties, and to my sister and parents for their excitement about this Element.

*This Element is dedicated to my empathetic, smart, and funny
teenager for the kisses and laughter.*

Cambridge Elements

Political Psychology

Elements in the Series

In Defense of Ideology: Reexamining the Role of Ideology in the American Electorate
Elizabeth N. Simas

Issue Publics: How Electoral Constituencies Hide in Plain Sight
Timothy J. Ryan and J Andrew Ehlinger

Stronger Issues, Weaker Predispositions: Abortion, Gay Rights, and Authoritarianism
Paul Goren

Empathy and Political Reasoning: How Empathy Promotes Reflection and Strengthens Democracy
Lala Muradova

A full series listing is available at: www.cambridge.org/EPPS

For EU product safety concerns, contact us at Calle de José Abascal, 56–1°,
28003 Madrid, Spain or eugpsr@cambridge.org.